A Woman Tenderfoot in Egypt

Also from Westphalia Press
westphaliapress.org

A Woman Tenderfoot in Egypt

1920s Travel Recollections

Grace Thompson Seton

WESTPHALIA PRESS
An imprint of Policy Studies Organization

Westphalia Press
An imprint of Policy Studies Organization
1527 New Hampshire Ave., NW
Washington, D.C. 20036
info@ipsonet.org

ISBN-13: 1-63391-354-6
ISBN-10: 978-1-63391-354-7

Cover design by Taillefer Long at Illuminated Stories:
www.illuminatedstories.com

Daniel Gutierrez-Sandoval, Executive Director
PSO and Westphalia Press

Updated material and comments on this edition
can be found at the Westphalia Press website:
www.westphaliapress.org

A
WOMAN TENDERFOOT
IN EGYPT

BY

GRACE THOMPSON SETON

Author of "A Woman Tenderfoot," "Nimrod's Wife," etc.

ILLUSTRATED

JOHN LANE, THE BODLEY HEAD Ltd.
LONDON, VIGO STREET, W. MCMXXIII

THE AUTHOR
At the Temple of the Sphinx

To
THE POET
MY FELLOW-TRAVELLER
AND TO ALL WOMEN WHO HAVE THE VISION

WHAT THE AUTHOR SAYS TO
THE READER

L'Envoi

Mais les vrais voyageurs sont seulement ceux qui partent,
Pour partir, coeurs légèrs, ressemblant aux ballons,
De leur fatalité jamais ils ne s'écartent,
Mais, sans savoir pourquoi, disent toujours,
>> Allons!
>> *Baudelaire.*

The S. S. Adriatic glided pridefully through New York
Bay, nosing to Sandy Hook. I waved a cheerful hand to
the Statue of Liberty, and rejoiced that I was not permanently stuck on a granite base, but could follow the
will o' the wisp of the true traveller and, like Baudelaire's
chronic voyageur, with a heart as light as a balloon, not
seek to escape my fate. Unlike the jolly tourist, however, who travels for travel's sake, my journey had a
purpose.

It was to renew acquaintance with a land old in story
and in emotion. Ten years of water had gone under the
memory bridge since the land of Ammon-Ra and of the
Pharaohs had spread its lure about me.

Therefore to Egypt I would go. But to a modern
Egypt, as well as the ancient—to know people this time,
rather than places, as an observer rather than a traveller.

The "unearned increment" was great, for I crossed
the trail of a world figure, the Conqueror of Palestine,

WHAT AUTHOR SAYS TO READER

Field Marshal Viscount Allenby, now arbiter of Egypt, and I was permitted to watch other threads weaving important figures in the great tapestry of world history—especially that complex picture of womanhood in Egypt, shot through with the crimson and gold outlines of the Militant and of the New Woman, as represented by Mme. Zaghlul Pasha and Mme. Schrauri Pasha. So that is why this book is offered to those whose egos permit them to be interested in the other person.

My sincere thanks and appreciation are herewith extended to all the gracious persons of every color-thread in this slice of Things as I Saw Them, from queen to peasant, from administrator to government clerk, who offered a helping hand to unravel the tangle of modern life.

GRACE THOMPSON SETON

Greenwich, Conn., 1922.

CONTENTS

ILLUSTRATIONS

ILLUSTRATIONS

BOOK I

EGYPT TODAY

PART I

ON-THE-RIVER-THAT-FLOWS-UP-STREAM

A WOMAN TENDERFOOT
IN EGYPT

CHAPTER I

EGYPT YESTERDAY AND TODAY

A T last again I saw approaching the shores of Alexandria—the gateway to that country of my most inviting memories—Egypt.

The Adriatic was the first ship since the Great War to bring tourists on a peace footing. For seven long years had the pleasure travel service been interrupted, and hordes of hungry porters and dragomen awaited us, eager for our gilded blood. Not even the petty annoyances and delays of landing, and of luggage-inspection—for the barrage of war-regulations of a country still under martial law had not lifted—could rob me of the Egypt thrill.

One gets out of Egypt, as elsewhere, pretty much, what one puts into it. If your magic carpet is spread to catch the beauty, the history, and the mystery of a race, which for eighty centuries has contemplated death, and has striven to arrest the swing of the universe, then, one may learn something of the spirit of this unique people; something of their belief that immovable Nature endures among all her changing forms, that the soul survives as an individual entity, even as the cosmic phenomena survive the passing ages.

[1]

A WOMAN TENDERFOOT IN EGYPT

The art of the ancient Egyptians is one long poem to death—their statues, monuments, temples, all portray what a great prophet so well expressed at a later time: "In the midst of life we are in death." Therefore, Egypt destroyed nothing, but sought by all the arts of the priestly occultist and the skilled artisan to preserve the body and the material accessories. From before the dawn of history, Egypt has perpetuated herself. Envision her down through the ages—her millions of mummies reverently buried in her soil, surrounded in the darkness by their pottery, food utensils, jewelry and religious vessels; all symbols of the pleasure-pain, the soul-heart of this endless human scroll. Nothing has been lost. What is visible today is but a fragment of yesterday.

The lion-headed goddess, Sekhmet, sculptured in the fourteenth century B. c., by some nameless artist-workman, in whom had descended the skill of generations, has always seemed to me the most living symbol of ancient Egypt. With what infinite skill has the massive, cruel, lion head been placed upon a body that typified the highest fruitful form of nature—Woman. In her hand, with great dignity, she holds the lotus-bud sceptre of the spirit. Charm, beauty, ruthless power, emanate from her black granite lines. Her feet are planted firmly upon the soil which sustains her. That soil was made up of the bodies and lives of the *fellaheen*, those myriads of peasantry without which Egypt would be as naught. The artisan fashioned her marvellous proportions, only the priests knew the occult meaning of her lion head. Elie Faure thus phrases the power of the Priest over his artists and his rulers: "Master of the Soul, or at least holding by

[2]

the wrist the hand that expresses it, the Priest permits all things to the King, and the King permits all things to the Priest."

The Priests and the Priest Kings, as such, have passed away, but the body of Egypt, like the goddess Sekhmet, throughout the ages has remained the same—an indestructible, classically-beautiful, productive force, which, as always, is sustained and nourished by the mass of unthinking, hard-working peasantry, who have little or none of the philosophy and education of the governing lion-headed upper classes.

If one has not a magic carpet, but a newspaper-bred desire for facts, and a *flair* for news, he will put Egypt aboard the International Limited which is making a world tour just now, gathering up the old lamps of established governments and exchanging them for new. There is already a lively company on this changing hurly-burly of nations. China, a republic, is there, and Germany going through the motions of being one. Japan, though still hugging her ancient lamp of Empire, is there, not wishing to be out of any world show. Italy, too, though for the present she is safe with the increase in the popularity of the Royal Family resulting from the calling to power of the everywhere acclaimed Fascisti.

Of course the whole mince-pie of Middle Europe, and that foot-ball of the powers—Turkey—are there, and hectic Ireland and, finally, that crowning example of autocratic lamp extinction—Russia, very busy being burnt with her fiery new lamp of Bolshevism—take some of the best seats.

In the following chapters I shall relate what one woman saw of Egypt's struggle to join this none too restful com-

[3]

pany of world all-star vaudevillians. Egypt, poor dear, stalks on the stage as a tragedienne. Her "political number" drips with strife and sorrow and disappointed hopes. But, fortunately, she has another side to tell us, which is full of promise and inspiration. Education has volplaned over the Mediterranean and landed firmly on her Nile banks. She is not only beginning to think, with her lion head, but her arms and legs are losing their classic immobility, and the new life is extending down to the very soil, where the soul of the *fellaheen* is becoming articulate. Ancient Egypt is dead; but modern Egypt is alive—and thinking.

CHAPTER II

WHERE Blue Nile meets White Nile may be seen that strange struggle of the Waters when a river flows up stream. The rains on the Abyssinian tablelands drain into the Blue Nile and its tributary, the Atbara, from June till September, which causes a volume of water, sometimes as high as 350,000 cubic feet per second or even more, to flow down to the junction of the Bahr-el-Gebel and the Sobat and pen up their waters in the White Nile Valley.

This terrific sport of the Nile gods during August and September furnishes a water battle of impressive grandeur. The Blue Nile God spreads his huge fluidic body against the White Nile God, who, outflanked, as well, is pushed back steadily, slowly, irresistibly along his own line of march. The White Nile must of necessity be overpowered and forced to retreat. For weeks the battle is drawn out, a veritable struggle of Titans, and then the weakening forces of the Blue Nile allow his ever-persistent neighbour to become his friend, to follow his natural course, and to flow down upon the exhausted Waters of the Blue Nile and to nourish anew its valley.

This remarkable river, the Nile proper—from the Ripon Falls at Lake Victoria to its five finger outlets into the Mediterranean Sea—is the longest single stream in the world. Upon its banks, made fertile by its life-

[5]

giving powers, is a strip of reclaimed desert from five to fifteen miles in width, which has nourished all the curious and vivid peoples which have ruled Egypt and been ruled by her, and who have left monuments of their greatness in the living rock and in the changing, yet changeless, sand. The glory of Thebes, of Memphis, is in its past. Alexandria faced its sunset long ago. Despoiled of its treasures, it borrows a popularity for those who seek relief, upon its damp and foggy shores, from the blistering heat of an Egyptian summer. Today the brain, if not the heart, of Egypt, is Cairo.

Cairo! What does it mean to the traveller who has stayed long enough to assimilate first impressions and to see beneath the surface of its life?

No city is more cosmopolitan, more rich in sharp contrasts of people, places and customs.

Before the "disturbances" of recent years, Cairo had more newspapers than London or New York. There were newspapers in English, French, Italian, Syrian, Greek, Arabic, and a variety of native dialects. Of course many of these had a very limited circulation; and now a number of them have been suppressed.

The Esbekiyeh and the Muski are the same, the native foods are the same, as a thousand years ago when Gohar conquered Egypt, for his master, the Fatimite Muizz, and founded the new Capital of Cairo in 969: and four years later, after conquering Syria, the Great Muizz,—Moses—himself, came to the new city and lived there for two years until his death. Spices and saffron and sandal are still brought by caravan along the desert routes. Meal is still pounded by a hand pestle, and silk and cotton and wool are woven on hand looms. The

[6]

mosques still hold their *Kuttabs*, the native schools, in groups of squatting, chanting boys who surround a teacher-priest and drone out the *Surehs* of the Koran, and labour over the elementary schooling which the *fiki* gives them, none too gently.

Even so, "Old Cairo" is changing with astonishing rapidity. "Flats" are being remodelled. Bathrooms and dining-rooms and kitchens, with European stoves, are no rarity, while New Cairo, along the Sharia-el-Manakh and the quarters of Ismailiyeh and Tewfikiyeh are built and furnished European fashion.

The new suburb of Heliopolis is connected with Cairo by trolley lines. It has wide boulevards, modern shops and apartment houses, and a huge modern hotel which was used during the Great War for a Military Hospital, but which is now being refurnished up-to-date.

Down by the River Bank, the long, picturesque masts of the cotton boats, lined up to be unloaded, form a forest of dead timber, silhouetted against a modern, iron, railway bridge. The style of this river craft has not changed since the Pharaohs, nor the costume of the river men. Over the bridge, however, roll modern freight and passenger cars, carrying people whose clothes show no distinguishing mark from the usual civilized garb. Unless it be an occasional Tarbush, the native fez.

The principal shops on the Place de l'Opera and neighbouring streets are modelled after the Bon Marchè in Paris or Harrod's in London, and the smaller shops suggest those of the rue de Rivoli, or of Oxford Street.

If one wants to see squalor and misery and disease, it is here, as in any great city. If one wants to see beauty and a brilliant social and civic life, it is here, also, in abun-

[7]

dant proportion among the Egyptian natives. In the English and American Colonies one can live, if one chooses, a life entirely conforming to the accustomed standards of these nations. One can be busy from morning till night, and till the next morning, with polo, tennis, luncheons, teas, dinners, dances, and never see the inside of a mosque, or tomb, or bazaar, nor hear a word of Arabic or of French, which is the language of the cultivated Egyptian society.

The charm of Cairo to the traveller from the Occident, is that very novelty of experience which he cannot find at home; and the sophisticated, even blasé, attitude of many English residents strikes the traveller as a false note. One must remember, however, that for them, Egypt means a career, not a novelty.

Since the Nile was first made possible to the casual tourist by Mr. John Mason Cook in 1870, thousands of entranced sightseers have negotiated the Temples and Tombs, from Cairo to Assouan and learned the names and dates, and places.

This is not a guide-book for the tourist, but a kaleidoscope of People and of Animals and Things, Animate and Inanimate. Like me, you will be jumped from Cairo to Luxor overnight, and back again, with never a stop at a temple, not because the temples should be skipped, far from it, but because, like me, you have already "done them" and are now seeking the impressions of Modern Egypt, the Egypt that is seething with revolution and change.

In the Cairo of today are to be found some of the most dynamic personalities on the World's Stage. They are making history.

[8]

CAIRO, ON THE RIVER NILE

The Conqueror of Palestine is there—England's example of a hero—Field-Marshal Viscount Allenby, a Fujiyama among men, dominating the picture. The Revolutionist-Patriot, the idol of Egypt, is there, Saad Zaghlul Pasha. Or rather he is represented now, in his exile, by his wife, Sophia *hanem,* a woman who would be remarkable in any country, a leader of men as well as of women. There is Mme. Charaoui Pasha, a Moslem noblewoman who is the head of the New-Woman Movement in Egypt, which is striving to play a large part in the advancement and welfare of the country.

The Cairene stage is crowded with interesting foreigners and with the still more interesting Egyptians, who are bravely putting up a losing fight for the political independence of their country. Some of these I was fortunate enough to meet, and they will be considered next, as, in telling their story, I am giving the picture of changing Egypt, political and social, as I saw it: and it also gives the necessary background for the problem which Lord Allenby, the Arbiter of Egypt, is working out.

BOOK I

PART II

FATIMA AS SHE IS TODAY

I

THE NEW WOMAN

CHAPTER III

WOMEN LEADERS OF MODERN EGYPT

EVER since the gorgeous time of the despotic Pharaohs when a certain princess responded to the call of curiosity and of compassion, and drew up the infant Moses from his hiding-place among the bulrushes to a life of ease in the palace *harîm*, and Cleopatra used her lithe body and languorous eyes to change the destinies of men and nations, women have meddled with the affairs of government and caused the Recording Angel to start another sheet in the ledger.

Of all the most unlikely places—at the top of Africa—the New Woman has arrived. She crept into Egypt as far back as 1911 and organized, with several hundred members, "La Femme Nouvelle" (literally, the New Woman).

She developed an even more progressive step in 1919 when a group of women, having suffered much in the present struggle which Egypt is making for greater political freedom, formed themselves into the "Ladies' Delegation for the Independence of Egypt," usually called the "Ladies' Wafd." They are pioneers, the Susan B. Anthony, the Anna Howard Shaw, the Inez Milholland of Egypt.

The New Woman has entrenched herself in the Upper, or Pasha, class of Egyptians, Mohammedan as well as the Christian Copt. She has spread through the mid-

[13]

dle, or *bourgeois* class, by means of the spirit of emulation and the power of education, and she has even
penetrated to the *fellaheen,* or peasants, where the possession of money has developed ambition.

In Egypt, as all over the world, there is a shifting of
social frontiers between the classes, so that one cannot
place the New Woman, except, broadly, among the women
of education, or wealth, or those possessing both of these
mollifiers of life's thorny path.   Recent opportunity enabled me to study first-hand these various aspects of
"the New Woman" which are here given; while in an
another chapter, I shall relate my adventures with "the
Other Woman."   She, also, as yet little touched by the
New Woman movement, forms an interesting group—the
fellaheen, including the rich *fellah* (peasant) woman,
the Bedouins, the *bourgeoisie,* of lesser degree—upon
which the labours of the educators, the American, French
and native, mission and school teachers, are beginning to
blossom through a sterile land.

How is Egypt modern, and why should there be Women
Leaders?

Why should some women in Egypt have stepped out
of their *harîms* and, dangling their veils beside them, be
working day and night to bring independence to their
country—a true independence as they see it, both political and social?

To answer this politically, one must go back a little
into Egypt's history.

To answer it socially, one has only to know that the
world-wave of self-determination began to lap the mental shore of educated Egypt about ten years ago, and has
been gathering in volume ever since receiving great

impetus during the Great War. It has swept over con-·
ventions and inhibitions, of women as well as men, and
has carried with it the various forms of civic progress—
schools, hospitals, dispensaries, welfare, hygiene and
sanitation.

It is now forty years since England first took a hand
in straightening out Egypt. Her grip has tightened and
eased up and tightened again in a long series of acts under a few wise administrators of exceptional ability, Lord
Cromer, Lord Kitchener and Lord Allenby. Tremendous
have been the improvements for Egypt accomplished by
these Englishmen. Oppression relieved, laws made and
Law Courts established where even the peasant could
find protection; trade encouraged, commerce developed,
especially along the line of Egypt's great staple, cotton;
the Assouan Dam completed and, by that triumph of
engineering skill, the opening-up for agriculture of great
tracts of desert adjacent to the Nile; various dispensaries
and hospitals for the relief of suffering—all this the
English have done and more.

Going along with these benefits, and the one that must
be considered the greatest of them all, as a factor in the
present "political unrest," is the changing social condition due to the advance of Education. The teaching by
the printed word has brought to Egypt the world—what
it is doing and feeling. It has unleashed the power of
thought and expression throughout the upper and middle
classes and has filtered down to the peasants, whose
patient toil is the wealth of Egypt. The credit for the
spread of Education, however surprising it may seem,
must be given largely to the efforts of the French and
American missionaries, which began over sixty years ago.

[15]

A WOMAN TENDERFOOT IN EGYPT

No intelligent Egyptian, and certainly none of the Zaghlulists, as the adherents of the Independent Nationalists, or "Democratic Party," are familiarly called after their leader, deny the benefits that England has worked in Egypt. But the itch for independence has spread like a fever through all classes. Even as a child, brought up and educated by its parent, seeks to throw off his stern discipline—so the Nationalists are struggling to throw off the governing hand of England. Through the High Commissioner's intercession, this has been accomplished in part. On March 16, 1922, the British Protectorate was withdrawn, with the martial law, rendered necessary by the War, which had been in the land more or less for seven years. And the Sultan was graduated into King of "the Kingdom of Egypt," which was declared "a sovereign independent state."

Meanwhile the real leaders of this strange land of the Nile, Saad Zaghlul Pasha, and the group around him, were banished to the Seychelles Islands in the Indian Ocean, and they remained banished. Zaghlul Pasha has since been transferred to Gibraltar.

Meanwhile Egypt looked with suspicion upon a King and a Premier and his Cabinet, which were set up by the British and did not represent the will of the people; and Egypt "quieted down" only in the newspapers. The political agitation went on; the women for the first time took a hand in public affairs. They were the wives, daughters and sweethearts of the banished leaders who formed a militant political group with other leaders in the larger New Woman movement.

It will be a surprise to most readers of the Occident to see these women in conventional clothes and to realize

[16]

that, instead of being bejewelled and pampered dolls, or sad-eyed slaves, they have broken out of *purdah* (seclusion of woman) and are using all the modern methods both for their political opposition and for their general welfare work.

CHAPTER IV

LET us first consider the most picturesque aspect of the New Woman, the militant political group, the "Ladies' Wafd (Delegation) for the Independence of Egypt." It is composed of women drawn from the ever-widening circle of the New Woman who is demanding her "place in the sun," from West to East, around this whirling world of ours. Whether history writes the record of these women as political agitators, or inspired patriots, their work is none the less remarkable, and especially in a country where woman has always been suppressed and considered the chattel of man: where, until recently, she has been hidden out of sight and not so much as the mention of her name been allowed in public.

Inspired by a deep patriotism which suppression has brought to the point of fanaticism, these women work for the release of their leader, Saad Zaghlul Pasha, and for the men who have been exiled with him. Also for those who are prevented by prison walls from carrying on their efforts to break down the power of the British, and of the Zarwat Ministry. They claim that the present Government, under King Fuad I, and his Cabinet, does not represent the Egyptian people:—that the Premier Zarwat Pasha is not even an Egyptian, but a Tunisian, and that his cabinet consists of men from the old Pashadom, or titled class, which the British suppressed because of their exploitation of the lower classes, especially the *fellaheen,* or peasants; that, now, the whole vicious circle is in being again; that the Egyptian people will be judged by these men; and that the precious opportunity to show that the Egyptians can govern themselves will be lost, because the only men who, they say, are the real leaders of Egypt, with Saad Zaghlul Pasha at their head, are banished, imprisoned and suppressed by the stern use of Britain's superior power.

On the other hand the case is not so simple. A long presentation of it is not germane here, but it must be remembered that Egypt has a remarkable soldier and statesman, one of the world figures today, the conqueror of Palestine, adjudicating the case of England and Egypt. Field Marshal Viscount Allenby, G.C.B., G.C.M.G., etc., so far as possible, considering all the varied interests involved, has shown himself sympathetic to the Egyptian National aspirations. For over three years he tried to treat with the Independent Nationalists, but he found the attitude of Saad Zaghlul Pasha so uncompromisingly "Egypt for the Egyptians," and the fiery spirit of rebellion and reprisal so strong, that he finally had to banish Zaghlul Pasha to Malta, then permitted him to reside in Paris and, finally, after two years, to return to Egypt. On this occasion, in the autumn of 1921, Egypt gave Zaghlul Pasha a tremendous ovation. But soon the old friction produced more serious riots, and the measures used by the British to suppress these attacks on life and property resulted in further reprisals by the Egyptians, who took a "life for a life" in the struggle to free their country from foreign domination. The Zagh-

[19]

lulists would agree to no compromise proposals, but insisted upon a complete British abdication. This, Lord Allenby, acting for England, was not prepared to do, on account of British interests, of the foreign interests, and of the Suez Canal, and, above all, because Egypt having been dominated by one foreign power or another for so many hundreds of years it was only fair to ask her to demonstrate her ability to establish a wise self-government before removing all her protection and throwing her into the "dog-fight of nations." Still, Lord Allenby realized that, to phrase it in the words of a high official: "It is against modern thought to hold fourteen millions of people against their will, . . . and very expensive." He found he was able to treat with the "Moderates," and Sarwat Pasha is reported to have said that he could form a cabinet if Zaghlul were out of the way. In the interests of peace Zaghlul was again banished, with some of his lieutenants.

Here it is that the women, whose photographs are shown for the first time, stepped into the limelight. These photographs are snap-shots taken for home use only and are in no case flattering. It is a great innovation to permit the picture of a Moslem woman of high degree to be published at all, and, so far as I know, it is the first time any such have been reproduced. The permission to use them was given me, because these Oriental women want American women, and also European, to know their side of their story, which hitherto has never been told. They want to take their place in the world. For this reason they have broken through the tradition of ages and accepted publicity "as American Ladies do."

Women when roused to action have ever been more

single-minded than men, and the fire of spiritual rebellion is in the heart of every woman in the Zaghlulist Party. The treatment meted out to her loved ones and to her Egypt, the military suppression of what she considers her just and proper rights, has crystallized the martyr-spirit in her.

All this means that, lifted out of the norm, women are capable of supreme sacrifice and of unflagging, undeviating concentration for an idea. It explains the tremendous gulf that has been bridged between the Oriental recluse of yesterday and the modern militant.

Who is the leader of this Ladies' Delegation?

It is a Mohammedan lady of high birth, the wife of Egypt's banished leader, Madame Saad Zaghlul Pasha and the most remarkable woman of Egypt. Sophia *hanem* (Lady Sophia) is the daughter of Mustapha Pasha Fahmi, who was Prime Minister for fifteen years under the Khedive Abbas Hilma II, and the wife of Saad Zaghlul, the lawyer who has raised himself from the peasant class to the exalted rank of Pasha. *Pasha* corresponds roughly to the English title of "Lord," as *Bey* does to "Sir." Saad Zaghlul Pasha was made Minister of Education by Lord Cromer, then High Commissioner of Egypt, who prophesied for him "a career of great public usefulness." Saad Pasha, as he is affectionately known, has become by virtue of his fiery patriotism, his great gifts of oratory, and knowledge of mass psychology, the accepted leader of the Egyptian people.

When Zaghlul Pasha, President of the Egyptian Delegation, was permitted to return from his first banishment, Egypt roared itself hoarse with a hundred-mile cheer from Alexandria to Cairo. The train was held back by human hands, so great were the crowds all along the railroad. The Egyptian Mail, on April 6, 1921, described the event in Alexandria as "A Record Ovation for Lord Zaghlul."

"Behind a cyclist detachment came a procession of motor cars. The first, a closed car (Ali Bey Fahmi's, if I am not mistaken) was completely covered with flowers, and inside a veiled lady acknowledged the frenzied cheering of the crowd, saluting with both hands. She was Madame Zaghlul Pasha.

"Many other Egyptian ladies followed, peering out from their cars at the amazing scene. There were detachments of Boy Scouts. There were groups of Girl Guides, in dark blue dresses, white floating veils and red ties.

"In Alexandria a dance was also given in honour of Madame Zaghlul Pasha at the house of Gafar Fakhri Bey to which many ladies of the highest Egyptian families were invited."

These extracts show, as well, the changing times. Ladies appearing in public scenes and at a dance with men, other than their relatives, and even Boy Scouts and Girl Guides in northen Africa!

Sophia *hanem* is today the power behind the Zaghlulist party. In 1896, at the age of twenty, she married Saad Pasha, who is many years her senior, and when he was arrested the second time, on December 23rd, 1921, she grasped his falling mantle and draped it over her *habara* and her veil. She said:

[22]

MADAME ZAGHLUL PASHA

"Saad Pasha lives—is here—so long as I, his wife, am here."

Men, as well as women, throughout Egypt look upon the Zaghlul home in Cairo, popularly called the "House of the Nation," as the Mecca of their hopes and aspirations.

All the Coptic *Evelyns* and *Moneeras* and the Moslem *Fatimas*, *Sophias* and *Ayeshas* up and down the Nile, are praying for their country's "True Independence," and pouring this thought upon the woman who now represents them. Surrounded by a group of women, whose relatives have shared her husband's exile, Saad Zaghlul Pasha leads an extraordinary life for any woman of any country.

I was told that it would be most difficult, if not impossible, to see her. Realizing that I could hope for little assistance on the part of my British or American friends, official or military, I wrote to her, as from one woman to another, that as one who had worked for the greater freedom of women in my own country I hoped she would allow me to meet the woman who was doing so much to help the cause in Egypt, and suggested a time when I could call upon her. Not daring to trust the dragoman to deliver this missive, and having been warned that I must proceed most carefully in order not to become "an international complication," I set out forthwith to deliver it myself. With the use of a friend's motor car, we in due course came to Sharia (Street) Kasr-el-Eini, where Madame Zaghlul lives, not more than two stones' throw from the Egyptian War Office, and stopped before a comfortable mansion surrounded by a small garden, laid out formally, but relieved by the feathery foliage of the pepper trees and the rich shining leaves of the rubber plants. A motley crowd of a hundred or more men of the poorer class loitered near the entrance gates of wrought-iron. While I watched the dragoman give the note to a responsible party, I saw fifteen or twenty women arrive in motors and carriages (*arabiyeh*) and go into the house. Some were veiled; others wore black satin gowns or modern coloured dresses and hats of evident French make. These last were Copts, or Christians. Evidently there was a Woman's Meeting of some importance going on. •

On the third day, a very polite reply, in excellent English, making an appointment, was received from a bearer. Although the telephone is now installed in the principal shops and to some extent in the homes, it is not the guide, philosopher and friend that we know, and the custom of "chit" sending is still prevalent.

What did I expect to find when I duly presented myself at the "House of the Nation" at Insha? A vision, perhaps, of gorgeous houris, languishing, cross-legged, on cushions, around a marble fountain: some one tinkling a *nakkareh*, or making other native music while the *Shâ ïr*, the singer story teller, spun yarns of bygone heroes or new-made love affairs; and, surely, a cockatoo and a gazelle upon the marble floor. Instead my eyes rested upon a modern interior, furnished in French fashion with Oriental touches, a conventional drawing-room fitted with fine rugs, gold and silver brocades and carved furniture, and, in the midst of it all, a slim, middle-aged woman of fragile body, but dauntless spirit. And, at the door, in place of the traditional guardian, there was a neat, up-to-date maid.

[24]

THE LADIES' WAFD

Madame Zaghlul Pasha is of medium height. She has iron-grey hair, waved and tastefully arranged; brown eyes that look introspective, a pointed nose, and rather thin lips, set in an oval face with fair skin—a lovely intellectual type of woman. She glided into the room and took a seat in her little court of women waiting to see her.

Those in the earnest group about her grew excited at times in the rehearsal of their country's troubles, but Sophia *hanem* never lost her firm and gracious dignity; her voice was never raised; her face at all times reflected the calm, almost placid, expression of a soul who had seen the Truth and who would follow it unswervingly to wherever it might lead.

"I am a prisoner in my own home," she said, "bound by my own will, Saad is a prisoner in Seychelles, but I keep myself here, his second self, his wife, and take his place."

When Zaghlul Pasha was arrested in his own courtyard on December 22, 1921, after having refused to retire to his estates in the country, his wife witnessed the military dispersal, with its inevitable bloodshed of a rebellious and fighting crowd which surged around the house demanding Zaghlul's release. She remained calm, gave necessary orders and then, alone, drove out along the road to the Great Pyramids of Gizeh.

With gracious composure she received the demonstrations of the native sympathizers along the streets, and "having thought it out," the decision came that she must stay and carry on the work, that, in spite of her husband's need of her, Egypt's need was greater. A momentous

[25]

decision for a Moslem lady wearing the *habara* and following the life of the *purdah*. She went to the telephone and with that quiet, though dynamic spirit, characteristic of her, rang up the Residency and asked to see the British High Commissioner. A secretary answered that he was out. She said: "No matter, you will do; I intend to remain. Convey the message to Lord Allenby." The voice asked whether she would speak French or Arabic, whereupon she changed to her native tongue and the staccato gutturals of Arabic conveyed this meaning:

"Tell His Excellency that I shall stay in Cairo; I shall do all in my power to take my husband's place. You may banish the body but you cannot banish the spirit of Saad Pasha. It still lives and in his own house, I, his wife, will be Saad until his return; for you cannot keep him away long, the people will not allow it, and even though he die, others will come, a never-ending stream. I shall do all in my power to excite this spirit of revolt for the Independence of Egypt—that is all I have to say."

Within an hour came a courteous letter from the High Commissioner, stating in the very best French that Madame could accompany her husband if she so desired, that arrangements had been made to send him to "a salubrious place" and that an immediate answer was desired.

Sophia *hanem*, however, continued in her refusal and prepared a statement which was published widespread in the newspapers, urging respect for law and order and counselling against violence.

Thus, step by step, she has made her own decisions in

MADAME ZAGHLUL'S APPEAL IN ARABIC

لجنة الشبيبة المصرية التنفيذية لنشر دعوة للمقاومة السلبية واذاعة تراث الوفد المصرى

نداء حرم الرئيس

ابناء وطنى الاعزاء

أرادوا أن يسكتوا سعداً وصحبه فنفوهم ثم أرادوا أن يسكتوا من بقى من اعضاء الوفد فاحتفظوا ثم خافوا عاقبة مايفعلون فافرجوا من هؤلاء الاعضاء ولكنهم فى الوقت نفسه اكرهوا الضعف على ان تجبههم ليمتنع عليهم ان يخاطبوكم وبينما سعد وصحبه منفيون. وبينما الاعضاء الوفد معرومون هذا الحرمان من ان يخاطبوكم تظهر بينكم دعوة لوزير سابق باسم شروط قدمها لتأليف وزارة ويظهر بعض الذين ابدوا فى الاشهر الماضية حربه منك الامة نصراء لدعوته الجديدة . فبينا انهم بكل ذلك لا يريدون الا ان يخدعوكم فى نيابتكم ليحزحزحوكم من موقفكم الذى يسوء الانجليز ان تظلوا فيه . يريدون ان يلبوكم بقشور لائقة لها من الامانة التى اصابتكم ومن طلبكم الجلاء والاستقلال . يريدون ذلك . ويريده الموظفون البريطانيون ايضا فلا عجب ان يكون هؤلاء . وأولئك متضامنين

والان لم يكفهم ان ابعدوا من مصر سعداً وصحبه بل هم يريدون فوق ذلك ان يكون تيهم الى ارض مهجرة قاسية

ظنوا انهم كلا ابعدوا الثقة بينكم وبينهم أثأروهم عن قلوبكم وطوحوا الى النسيان ذكراهم . توهموا ذلك وأملوا ان نخمد الحماسة التى تتأجج فى صدوركم ويهبط اليأس بنوائكم فيهون اخضاعكم ويسهل تسليمكم

لم يكفهم ان يبزلوم عنكم حتى يريدوا ان يبزلوهم من العالم كله — ولماذا ؛ ولاى جريمة ؛ لانهم نادوا باسمكم وطالبوا باستقلالكم ولم يستعملوا فى ذلك الا السلاح السلمى سلاح الحق والاقناع

لئن كان سعد شيخا فاعلموا ان هذا الذى الذى لا يد من عزيمته . اعلا بهم من عزيمته الا شئ واحد هو ان يعلم ومما ماانكم اعترافكم الضعف ولو لحظة واحدة فتركتم للاعبين ان يلعبوا بموقفكم وحقوق هذا الوطن عليكم

ثبتوا اذن اقدامكم وانبذوا المجادعين من بين صفوفكم . وذودوا ذود الاباة عن استقلالكم واصبروا فقد قاربتم نهاية الطريق وانتم فيها باذن الله ظافنون فائزون؟

صفية زغلول

٧ جادى الثانية سنة ١٣٤٠ — ٤ فبراير سنة ١٩٢٢

[27]

...ys so soon as the Company has the necessary equipment at its disposal.

Mme. ZAGHLUL'S APPEAL

Madame Zaghlul Pasha has issued the following appeal to the Egyptian nation:

"When I saw the troops surrounding the house and filling the garden to take away Saad, my inclination at first was to follow him wherever this force took him. But when I saw you killed, all my affection and feeling went out to you, and I felt from the bottom of my heart that I could not abandon you at such a critical time, and that my duty was to share your fate.

"If Saad needs my services, and he is in the greatest need of them now, I know that he approves my conduct and sacrifice, for he sacrificed everything quietly and with pleasure for the fatherland.

"My good children, you have proved that you are ready to give your blood to redeem the fatherland, if only to prove to the enemy that you are brave and prefer death to a life of slavery and humiliation. But the fatherland requires your blood and does not wish you to spend your energies; it wishes you to be wise and determined, it wishes you to be united, it wishes you to hold fast to your strong ties of brotherhood.

"Close up your ranks and ignore the English. Let their colony here be like an island separated from us by the sea of of their tyranny; but be hospitable, even in the hour of misfortune; protect our guests, and their houses and property; be their guards so as to outplay the measures of those who are not satisfied till they make trouble between us and our dear guests.

"We have no arms, but, when defending the fatherland, we are invincible and shall not be humiliated, nor can any power in existence subdue us.

"Courage, Egyptians! Let the fourteen million Egyptians be like one man, with one wish and one heart, working for the love of the fatherland and its prosperity, as well as to restore to it its independence.

"I have a request to make: Every Egyptian man and woman to remember, every morning, Saad and his noble colleagues. Let us all pray to the Almighty to restore those dear exiled ones to their sacred fatherland shining proudly in the bright sun of independence.

(Signed) SAFIA ZAGHLUL."

Madame Zaghlul Pasha has received a letter from her husband in which he says that his health is good, and that he approves the line of action she adopted.

THE PASHA'S DEPARTURE.

...ording to "Al-Mokattam" the "Fra...

[28]

a country where, traditionally, women's minds have been made up for them by either parents or husband.

So far as possible, Lord Allenby has pursued the clever policy of appeasement, and of ignoring Madame Zaghlul and all the whirl of activities of which she is a driving force. The most effective and far-reaching of these activities may now be considered.

"The Ladies' Wafd" helped to originate the boycott on English goods as a protest against the arrest and banishment of their leaders, and in demand for their return. Many prominent women of "La Femme Nouvelle" and of the "Mohammed Ali Society" worked with them; they felt that the first step towards reform was to "clean house" and to have "Egypt for the Egyptians"; that the present situation, with their leaders still banished, and foreigners over them, gave no opportunity to show the world that the Egyptians could rule themselves. They call the present status of Egypt the "false Independence."

Essentially modern were the methods used when the women started the anti-English boycott in January, 1922. They spared themselves neither time nor energy; a half-dozen began on the telephone, and by noon a squad of twenty women were out in their motors and carriages interviewing the principal shopkeepers of Cairo and Alexandria. As Mme. Zaghlul Pasha expressed it: "They have not had their hats off for a week." At first they were laughed at, but before a week had passed a delegation, this time of the shopkeepers, had waited upon the women and asked for their co-operation. They organized Women's Committees in the big cities and in the provinces, and recently held a meeting in Cairo of over

[29]

A WOMAN TENDERFOOT IN EGYPT

2,000 women who made political speeches and vowed continued effort to boycott the British and British goods. The story of their efforts calls to mind similar struggles in the last century in both England and America which started as Women's Rights and ended as Universal Suffrage. This phase of it, however, must necessarily be a later development, for at present the fire in their hearts is more for country, than for sex privilege.

The boycott affected the English merchants very seriously for several months, and then the change of governmental status, with Egypt declared a kingdom and the British Protectorate withdrawn, lessened public opposition. The merchants have been able to carry on a volume of business with foreigners which helps them to get on without the native trade. But there can be no doubt that the business of many firms was crippled much more than they are willing to admit. Some firms closed, some suspended business and others had liquidation sales.

Mme. Bahi-el-Dine Bey Barakat, member of a powerful family, is affectionately called "the soldier" by Mme. Zaghlul, "because she works so hard and is always on duty, and, now with this boycott on English goods, she gives all her energy and enthusiasm towards furthering our cause." She is a young person with lustrous eyes, set in a round face, with smooth dark skin and brilliant cheeks. When I saw her she wore the conventional head-dress of black silk, but the chiffon face-veil was dangling from one side. She had just come from an encounter with a shopkeeper, an English haberdasher. She was on the opposite side of the street when she saw two Egyptian gentlemen enter the English shop. At once she went across and addressed the two men in Arabic, asking them not to buy English goods. Picture this for a veiled Moslem lady, only 22, and pretty as well! The two Egyptians left their expensive purchases of neckties on the counter and walked away from the furious haberdasher.

For a veiled lady to address a man has hitherto been considered "shameful"; but country comes before custom, and the spirit of Joan of Arc is strong in the bosom of the New Woman in Egypt. It caused them to institute the modern street manifestations. The accompanying snap-shots show the first "protest parade" of women in the streets of Cairo, in 1919.

So swift has been the development that it is not an uncommon thing now for the *harîm* to stage a public manifestation in the streets of Cairo. In March, 1922, one of these consisted of 80 motor cars full of ladies, protesting against the exile of Zaghlul Pasha, martial law, Sarwat's ministry, and the "false Independence." The manifestation lasted two hours, the parading women went to every Consul-General, giving each a written protest. The King also came in for his share of protest.

On my first visit Mme. Zaghlul Pasha served native cakes for tea, saying: "You know, I buy nothing now, everything is made at home because of the boycott."

Sophia *hanem's* two nieces, Mme. Taher Bey el Lozi, and Mme. Amine Bey Youssef, two plump, well-favoured young women in the twenties, aid her in the work she has assumed. One of them coming into the room, gave the two salutes, first the affectionate one, a kiss on each cheek, then the one of respect which is to kiss the fore-

[31]

head and make a gesture with the forefinger of the right hand on nose, cheeks and chin. She presented some flowers. "These are from our garden, from father to you." "Ah," said Mme. Zaghlul, smilingly, "see how we women have progressed from *purdah*. I am being offered flowers by a gentleman."

"What is the future of the women here?" I asked.

"It is remarkable, the change. I was away two years and I could not believe the transformation in thought and action that I saw when I came back. We are going ahead very fast. My husband is very liberal about women's customs. The *habara* and veil are not part of our religion, you know. They will have to be done away with very soon, in a few years, perhaps a few months, not for themselves, but of what they represent. But they are very becoming and women will hate to part with them.

It is interesting to note that these progressive women, while they are blazing the trail for greater freedom, have no aversion to the *habara* and the veil, modified as the veil is now to a mere suggestion of face covering. They seem in no hurry to abolish it altogether, for they are essentially daughters of Eve. They consider it a badge of distinction, even as the Egyptian man wears a *tarbush*, a red felt cone, like a fez, at all times and places, and many of the Coptic women have voluntarily assumed the *boukra* which is the more refined form of veil used by the upper classes of Mohammedans. The peasant, and women of the minor *bourgeoisie*, wear the *yashmak* which is a rather coarse knitted piece of black silk, or cotton, or even a piece of solid cloth, usually held in place by a nose arrangement of gold, or brass. The lowest class, the *fella-*

[32]

heen women, while working in the fields rarely wear a
face-covering.

The *habara* consists of a light-weight material, usually
silk and always black, covering the head and shoulders,
and a strip of white crepe or chiffon, the *boukra,* quite
transparent, 7×10 inches, held in place by a loop over
the ears, thus being instantly removed or adjusted.
Mme. Zaghlul's had loops of gold. The still more mod-
ish, head-dress consists of a hat of white tulle with a
mere fold of tulle adjusted across the mouth. Very often
a smart French hat is worn with this chin-covering of
tulle, and so the veil is practically reduced to a symbol.
When these ladies travel abroad, as most of them do, the
"symbol" vanishes as soon as the steamer leaves Alexandria, not to be assumed again until its minarets are once
more in sight.

Mme. Zaghlul Pasha explained all this to me, with a
demonstration. With gracious simplicity she sent for
her *habara,* which she adjusted for my benefit, and for
two or three of her very smart French hats. Of one, a
toque of fine straw with circles of aigrette wisps, I remember having seen a copy in a Fifth Avenue shop. She
also adjusted the white tulle dress hat which had a fair-
sized brim and yellow roses. She was dressed in an up-
to-date French one-piece frock of blue-and-tan tricotine,
silk stockings, and high-heeled, strapped slippers. On
the street she puts over this in winter a long black coat of
velvet or sealskin, and in summer, a black, light-weight
skirt which is removed, with the *habara* in her home.

"What do you see as the future of your country?"
I asked.

"We shall struggle until Egypt is free!!" replied Sophia

hanem quietly. Our slogan is: *"Nous irons jusqu'au bout."* (We shall go on till the end.).

"Will your husband soon be released?"

A sad little shrug. "How can I tell? He is not a well man, far from it. He has a weak heart and has internal troubles, and he is not young.

"He sends word through the Residency that he is well and will have me think that he is comfortable in the Seychelles. I can only hope for the best, we are all believers in our God, whether Moslem, or Copts," turning to a Coptic caller, Mme. Wacyf Boutros Ghali, with one of those touches of affection that make Sophia *hanem's* followers worship her. A strong woman, and a lovable one; under the strange conditions of her life, she keeps a great heart and a shining spirit. When asked to describe her reception of delegations of men, which were so startling an innovation for a Moslem woman, Sophia *hanem* sent a servant to bring a beautiful cream scarf of transparent linen gauze, exquisitely embroidered, and a *galabeyeh,* the long native garment, of pure white silk, almost entirely covered with the finest drawn work. These she put on, and, causing a screen to be placed at the end of the large central hall of the mansion with an arm-chair behind it, she demonstrated how she received sometimes as many as forty men at once, and often two hundred a day. When the delegation is assembled she steps from behind the screen and talks to them passionately of the necessity of independence for Egypt. Her voice is clear and vibrant with feeling. She speaks from the heart, and often this frail woman has her listeners in tears. She is not veiled on these occasions but throws the white gauze over her head and around her throat to give a sem-

[34]

blance of it. This she does in order not to shock the ingrained habit of thought of her provincial male visitors. The fine sense of dramatization shown in staging this picture properly to me was unconscious, but, none the less, is one of the charms of this unusual woman, who has swept away one conventional barrier after another since she assumed the mantle of leadership which her husband was forced to lay aside.

Several mornings a week she presides over women's meetings where the machinery of the boycott, and other measures of the Zaghlulist party, are organized.

I was told that on May 16th each year a beautiful virgin was sacrificed to the Nile God—in propitiation to that exacting deity, that he may provide the water which must overflow the fields, and bring prosperity to Egypt. When I asked about this Mme. Zaghlul looked puzzled. Then, smiling gently, she exploded another myth I had been treasuring: "Oh, that was a Coptic rite, not Mohammedan at all, and is now practised only as a symbol. It is done in effigy. The sacrifice of a human being has not taken place for more than a hundred years."

The new order of things is demonstrated in the drawing-room of Sophia *hanem*. There all classes, from princess to peasant, can be seen drinking coffee, or tea, together, and there, one can study the New Woman in various aspects! I noticed a woman in peasant garb, sitting with her knees wide apart and her hands upon them and her feet planted firmly on the carpet. Occasionally some one addressed a remark to her in Arabic, when there came a ready response, and a smile. Evidently she could not follow the French phrases which shuttled back and forth through the room. She was dressed in the long

[35]

A WOMAN TENDERFOOT IN EGYPT

black costume and *yashmak* (a black knitted veil of
cotton) of her class, only cleaner, and wore most astonishing quantities of solid gold ornaments upon her
arms, chest, and even ankles. It has long been the custom for the peasant to bank her wealth upon her person
in this fashion. Of course the gold is convertible, but it
is rarely sold—the woman often denying herself comforts
to add to her weight of gold bands and coins. On her
forehead and chin were the blue lines tattooed, three on
chin, two on forehead, which are considered "smart" in
her class. She looked a sturdy sixty, but was probably
ten or fifteen years younger. The hard work and the
bearing of children begin so early in tropical countries!

She was Sitt Gaba. *Sitt* is a term of respect corresponding somewhat to the English "Mrs." or "Miss" or
closer still to the Japanese "San." She was a wealthy
woman of the *fellaheen,* who had travelled from her province up the river over a hundred miles, an innovation
for women of this peasant class, to offer her money and
her heart to Egypt's cause. Her wants are few, and
her income about $40,000 a year. The "rich peasant,"
as a class, really falls into Part II on "The Other
Woman," but individuals are filtering over increasingly into the New Woman Movement. Another
peasant woman on this occasion, who had seated herself
next to Mme. Zaghlul, has an income of $75,000 yearly.
She sipped her coffee neatly; and eagerly, but with
dignity, answered a remark which from time to time
was addressed to her in Arabic. Her neck and arms
and ankles also were weighted with many bands of solid
gold, and strings of gold coins tastefully assembled, hung
around her neck. Mme. Zaghlul's private income of

[36]

THE LADIES' WAFD

$40,000 to $50,000 is considered very modest.   Many of
the *fellaheen* have much more.   It is derived chiefly
from the land and the cotton crops.

My informant was an up-to-date young woman of title
from Alexandria, who further commented in fluent English upon the changed conditions: "Some of the peasants are rich, very rich, they have more money than we
have nowadays; that is, it seems so, for we are very ex-
travagant and they spend nothing, so they get richer and
richer.   Cotton was £40 during the War and now it has
been hammered down to £4 which makes us feel poor.
But the peasants will not have money long, if we cannot
have a really independent Egyptian Government.   You
know the present premier, Sarwat Pasha, and his Cabinet
belong to the old gang of pashas, who exploited the
people.   Every one, both high and low, knows that Saad
Pasha is a true, unselfish patriot, and a great statesman
too."

Her next remarks epitomized the attitude I found
in all the upper class homes; to an outsider, it seems a
case of "the pot calling the kettle black."

"The trouble is that the English do not know us. They
rarely know us socially for we, our own class, do not mix
with them.   They are very arrogant and snobbish.   The
attitude of the English Officials and their wives here is
amusing.   Mrs. £60 does not mix with Mrs. £30.   With
the exception of a handful at the top, who are they?   I
have been several seasons in London and have never met
any of them, or their families.   They come from
Margate, or the Provinces.   They are nobodies at
home and they have not the entrée to an exclusive
society here.   They know nothing about us and that is

why there are so many false stories circulated about us."

There is, of course, an adequate rebuttal on the English side. The British colonial policy of "not mixing socially" with foreign races is the result of long experience; but it should be said that the British officials often seem to entertain a real affection for the Egyptian men with whom they work.

The following are some of the other leaders in this militant group around Mme. Zaghlul. Madame Nift Ratib Pasha is a member of the "Ladies' Wafd" and of the Executive Committee of "La Femme Nouvelle," and is an indefatigable worker. One has only to look at that patient, determined, face with the full lips and almond eyes of the true Egyptian, to realize that her contributions to the women's activities are generous and tireless. Her *habara* is of charmeuse satin, though usually it is made of taffeta, and always black. She has pulled down the white chiffon veil, or, *boukra*, from its proper position over the nose. Quite often now the gauzy veil is draped below the nose, or even below the mouth.

As one looks at the face of Mlle. Aida Marcos Hanna, one cannot realize that behind this smiling exterior is a heavy heart. Her uncle and her fiancé are both exiled with Zaghlul Pasha. Mr. Makram Obeidthe is a very brilliant young man. He has been "Diplomatic Secretary" to several of the most distinguished Egyptians in the country and his knowledge and patriotic enthusiasm are safer simmering in the hot and humid Seychelles than boiling over into the affairs of the present Ministry.

Mlle. Aïda and her sister Mary are daughters of Marcos Hanna Bey, a prominent lawyer, and nieces of Sinnot Bey Hanna, the exile, whose wife and 19-year-old daugh-

MADAME ZAGHLUL PASHA

ter, Camille, I first met at the Boutros Ghali Palace in Faggala. They are always dressed in the height of the French fashion. Being Copts, that is, the native Christians, they do not wear "the veil," which is a distinctive Moslem custom. In a gentle, determined way, they are all active in political and welfare work. They speak wonderful English, and it was a relief to all concerned to give my sketchy and over-worked French a rest. Indeed, as French is the language of polite society among the Caireans and Alexandrians, a knowledge of the language is essential. Of course these women all speak Arabic, and many of them Italian and even English, although English is not popular among the Zaghlulists.

One often hears of the many Egyptians who have married foreigners, but the French wife of Wacyf Bey Boutros Ghali, and the American wife of Dr. Riad Fanous are the only two modernists who are prominent in the progressive movements. They are Sophia *hanem's* devoted helpers. Their sympathies seem absolutely bound up with the country into which they have married.

I had heard so much about the miseries of "mixed marriages," that I was interested to meet Louise Majorelly, wife of Wacyf Bey Boutros Ghali, who is a member of the "Democratic Party" and a writer of distinction, and who inherited a splendid position from his illustrious father, Boutros Ghali Pasha, one of Egypt's big men. This Egyptianized French woman proved to be a small and slender person, daintily gowned, but with a fiery spirit animating a butterfly exterior. If she was hiding a canker at her heart, she concealed it bravely. Her domestic and social life seemed to be exceptionally well-

[39]

favoured. She was the first to dispel the idea for me that all Egyptian men who could afford it must have several wives tucked away out of sight somewhere. So far as I was able to learn, not one of the large numbers of upper and middle class Egyptians whom I met, or heard about, had been asked to share her home with another wife.

The animating principle of Hilda Fanous, the young and enthusiastic Egyptianized American, was expressed when she said, her voice vibrant with feeling: "Do tell them in America about us; about these wonderful women who are seeking to restore Egypt's past glories. I am glad to feel that my lot is thrown in with them and proud to be able to work with them in the furthering of their ideals. And the men, they are wonderful, too. They are struggling to free their country from the shackles of ignorance and of foreign rule."

The sympathies of Hilda Fanous are entirely merged with the country into which she has married. Her husband, a native of Cairo, spent many years in America studying medicine and it was in Baltimore, the city of her birth, that Hilda at the age of 15, first met Dr. Riad Fanous, while he was a student of Johns Hopkins University. A few years later she married him in spite of strong opposition. Apparently she has seen no reason to regret her decision. Her father, Henry Hamm, still lives in Baltimore, and her brother Albert was in the aviation section of the United States Army during the war, while Hilda responded to the call of England and the Allies. In common with all these modern women, she qualified for nursing and stuck to the hospital work for over two years. She learned French in the Convent at Baltimore, and now has added Italian and Arabic.

She said, "Please correct the idea in America that we are barbarians, or even worse.

"Two ladies from Ohio forced themselves upon Mme. Zaghlul Pasha yesterday, when she was receiving her friends. They brushed past the astonished servant at the door, stood in the middle of the reception room, looked at us as though we were a circus, felt of the sofa pillows and window draperies to see if they were silk, and asked Mme. Zaghlul, 'How many wives has your husband?'; and seeming incredulous when she replied, after a stunned silence at the rudeness of it, 'My husband has no wife but me.' 'Have you any bathrooms?' was the next question, after they had exclaimed several times that they thought all Egyptians had as many wives as they could afford. They asked all kinds of rude questions and seemed to have no idea of the courtesy required in polite society. I was ashamed of the country of my birth."

The second most interesting Egyptian personality I met was Mme. Hoda Schrauri, a quiet-voiced Mohammedan lady. There is nothing about her to suggest the traits which have been so often associated in the western mind with the Egyptian *harîm* lady—over-fat, underdressed, lazy-minded in the manner of the traditional odalisque. This leader of women, in civic matters as well as political, has the silent strength of Egypt's great river, sweeping steadily forward. In the forties, with a grown daughter, behind her cultured and dignified exterior one realizes a clear brain and a determined will. I am almost afraid to say that she is beautiful. Her photograph gives very little idea of it, the satin com-

[41]

plexion, the large expressive eyes and the refined, though full, curves of her face. Her hair is dressed flat on the top and full behind, for the best effect of the *habara,* which she has just removed. In fact the universal beauty, the dark lustrous eyes, clear skins, and regular features, of these women, struck one with ever-increasing force. Any one who has been received in this society of women who have read much, thought much, speak several languages, discuss politics, down to the girl in her teens, must agree that there are more beautiful faces and voices to be met with among them than in any similar group among European or American circles. Mme. Schrauri Pasha's unusual charm and executive ability have made her not only President of the "Ladies' Wafd" but Honorary President of "La Femme Nouvelle." So definite has been her political stand, that her husband resigned the prominent post which he held under the Anglo-Egyptian Government. Her attitude is shown by the following *"Protest of Egyptian Ladies to Mr. Lloyd George, members of Parliament and all English newspapers,"* which she signed as President of the "Ladies' Wafd."

Against the banishment of Zaghlul Pasha, she wrote:—

"In supporting Sarwat Pasha's proposals Lord Allenby helps this ex-minister to return to power at the expense of the Egyptian people and renders the prospect of an understanding with Great Britain more hopeless than ever. The country finds these ambiguous proposals of such a nature as to maintain and aggravate the present atmosphere of mistrust which characterizes the relations between Egypt and Great Britain. How can we believe in the sincerity of an agreement which professes to recognize our independence

[42]

when the mouthpiece of our national aspirations has been struck for no other reason than demanding this independence?"

The following extract from a letter, hitherto unpublished, by Mme. Basima, wife of Astef Bey Barakat, is copied in her own English, and shows the quality of intelligence and education among these Moslem women leaders, as well as giving some of the occurrences, from the Egyptian point of view, which have produced the rapid development of independent action among women, causing them, veiled or unveiled, to parade the streets in protest, and even to make speeches in public, a thing unheard of five years ago. The author does not vouch for the truth of these statements. They are given to show the psychology which has caused so many women to break out of *purdah*.

Mme. Barakat wrote on January 18, 1922, to a friend in England who asked for news as the newspaper accounts were so contradictory:

"The people here have regarded the banishment of H. E. Saad Pasha Zaghlul and his friends as an insult to national dignity, and at once arose to express their disgust to that blind and blundering militarism. Schools in all parts of Egypt struck work, demonstrations in all parts of the country were made in which all classes took part—notables, emdehs, merchants, ulemas, advocates, doctors, engineers, students, government officials and all. Their cry of 'down with oppression,' 'We die that Saad might live,' 'Vive l'Egypte,' etc., resounded with vigour in an atmosphere charged with anger, wounded dignity and disgust. Government officials then struck work for three days. Lawyers, judges, courts, councils, and even merchants and coach-

[43]

drivers also struck work for three days. The military authorities distributed troops throughout the country. Demonstrations were suppressed with severity. Even a peaceful expression of opinion was not allowed. All gatherings were prohibited under threat of being fired at. . . .

"There could be but one result of these unjust measures; the nation to a man have rallied more closely round the sole patriotic Leader who has suffered and sacrificed his old age for the cause of the Country. There is another certain result. The despotic proceedings of the military authorities will simply add fuel to the fire of enthusiasm and patriotism that fills the hearts of all Egyptians. . . .

"As for us, we have resolved to live free or die honourably. We have learned to sacrifice life for the country and for the sublime principles of the Great Leader and his associates."

In a word, Sophia *hanem* has the supreme gift in a leader, that of inspiring others. Her immediate environment is quiet, but the quiet at the vortex of a maelstrom. To understand her work, one must know the activities of the Men's Delegation for the Independence of Egypt, which is conducting the affairs of the "Democratic Party," and also of her lieutenants—not only the "Ladies' Wafd," but the officers of the larger body, "La Femme Nouvelle."

Egypt wants to be free—free not only from England, but from ignorance and superstition—that is why there is a Zaghlulist party and why there are Women Leaders. They give their money, energy and heart to their Egypt and they rally to the support of the standards pulled

THE LADIES' WAFD

from the hands of their exiles, for "Men may come and men may go," but the ideal goes on forever. They want to restore their country's past glories—a country of unforgettable charm and endurance. In the words of Mme. Zaghlul Pasha: "The Egyptians are like their desert sand. You can walk over it and over it—but one day it rises up in a mighty storm and sweeps over you, and there is again—only sand and the desert."

CHAPTER V

LA FEMME NOUVELLE

WE will now consider the larger group of women who feel inspired to dedicate their lives to the cause of Egypt's freedom, not politically this time, but through the sounder agencies of education and civic development.

Once having opened the gate to modern methods, there is great opportunity for the women who wish to enter into the welfare and civic work of the nation, and many are already finding this wider expression, since there are both leisure and great wealth among the upper classes.

An interesting and important result of this larger life of the women has been the social unification of the two religions, which has been brought about by a common danger and a common enthusiasm. Our own great slogan "In union there is strength," is being applied with equal effect in the breaking-down of religious prejudice, so that, whether Moslem or Copt, the women are working together in all kinds of activities.

A glimpse of the activities of "La Femme Nouvelle" and of the "Mohammed Ali," which is another Moslem Women's Society organized to carry on welfare and civic activities, leaves one with the same impression as would a similar visit to Hull House in Chicago, or a settlement house in the Whitechapel district of London.

"La Femme Nouvelle" was well started before the

[46]

LA FEMME NOUVELLE

Great War, with several hundred members, both Moslems and Copts. It established Trade Schools and Dispensaries; also various Departments such as Education, Civics, Hygiene, Sanitation, and Playground. About $50,000 had been already subscribed for a Social Club House in Cairo to be modelled on the American plan. The ambition of this large body of women, who represent the brains, culture, and wealth of the country, is no less than to stimulate and control the welfare work of the whole nation. From the pulsating heart at Cairo, it proposes to send streams of new life to all the big cities of the Provinces and even to trickle into the Sudan.

I have a vivid recollection of being taken one morning to a street in the old quarter of Cairo in search of a sign in Arabic, meaning, the "Girls' Club of La Femme Nouvelle," which is really a school to prepare poor girls to earn a living. An old carved doorway admitted us to a large court-yard where a modern playground apparatus had been installed. The large house, a decayed old palace, belonging, I believe, to one of the wealthy members, was given over to various classes of instruction, in stenography and in the applied arts, suitable for girls. The girls are allowed to work at rug-weaving, embroidery, dress-making, lace-making and household work in order to learn a trade and become self-supporting. A proportion of the day is allotted to mental exercises when the girls are taught all the elementary branches, also simple hygiene, such as the care of teeth, eyes, skin and hair according to modern standards. About one hundred and fifty girls can be taken care of at a time and about half of them are generally boarders.

A WOMAN TENDERFOOT IN EGYPT

The active secretary of this school of "La Femme Nou-velle" is Mme. Gameela Abbia. She explained that the money for the organization work came from dues and yearly subscriptions. These varied, according to the size of the member's pocketbook, from one dollar a year to a thousand dollars—or more. Both democracy and co-operation are shown here! It is like the new town of the West which does not go through the tiresome stages of municipal illumination, first oil lamps, and then gas, but jumps from darkness into light, by means of an electric plant. The President of "La Femme Nouvelle," another modernist leader, is Mme. Amina, wife of Dr. Mahmoud Bey Sidky, who has cast aside her *habara* for a trip into Italy where the photograph reproduced here was taken. Most of the wealthy women of Cairo and Alexandria go to Europe in the summer. They pack away the silk and chiffon symbols and step out of *purdah* and do not re-turn to *la vie grotesque,* as they term their old life with the *habara* and veil until they land again upon their native shores.

Mme. Bey Sidky is a young matron who does much work in the larger field of women's activities, represented by "La Femme Nouvelle." This means she carries re-sponsibilities of the same relative importance as those of the President of the Women's Federated Clubs of Amer-ica or of the President of the National Woman's Suffrage Association in the "piping days" before the enfranchis-ing amendment.

Mme. Amina Sidky received me in her home one morn-ing, an apartment in the ancient quarter of old Cairo, and there I made the acquaintance of a chubby, lace-frocked, four-year-old toddler and a young gentleman

[48]

LA FEMME NOUVELLE

of a few months only, in charge of a native nurse. The drawing-room where, as usual, coffee and cake were served, was furnished in a "parlor set" of gilded wood work and pink brocade. Upon tables of agate and brass were photograph frames of mother-of-pearl inlay, and carved sandalwood. A very intelligent and charming personality is this wife of a prosperous physician in Cairo of the upper *bourgeois* class, a fine type of the New Woman who finds time in her active domestic and social life to conduct an important piece of welfare work.

Another Welfare Association has been established in connection with the Kasr-el-Aine hospital, where I spent many interesting hours of observation. It is composed of Moslem women, the "Wafd of Khalil Agha," and is doing much to alleviate suffering. It places foundlings, of which there are many; it aims to educate the native mother in more hygienic habits, and to induce women to use the maternity wards where they and their infants can be taken care of and taught new ways for the benefit of future Egypt. It is waging an especial war against flies and blindness. Dr. W. H. Kiep, the eye specialist at this Hospital, said that "In Cairo alone, according to the census there are more than 30,000 persons—one in twenty-six—who are blind in one or both eyes. In many towns and villages the proportion of sightless is greater, but the organized effort for hygienic education is helping."

The brilliant wedding in 1921, of one of Egypt's rich girls, is a good picture of the blending of the ancient Oriental customs with the new. Youssef Bey Ghali, a member of the "Men's Independent Wafd," was the groom;

[49]

the bride, a beautiful Egyptian Moslem of eighteen. This little Sophia spent $25,000 on her trousseau, not counting the resplendent jewels. Many more thousands attended the wedding at the Palace Boutros Gahi at Faggala in Old Cairo, in which the young people now occupy a modern suite of rooms, "parlor, bedroom and bath," done in the most luxurious French style. The feasting lasted many hours. Whole sheep and lambs were barbecued, a wealth of food dainties loaded the tables in a huge embroidered tent, set in the garden, and champagne flowed freely. The wedding guests, "ladies and gentlemen" together, please note, danced and made merry in the big house, while some of the old-fashioned Moslem women, congregated in a room upstairs and made the unusual request for "Saad Zaghlul Pasha," who was an honored guest, to visit them. This he did. There was much merriment and no woman veiled herself before him. This was both a tribute to the "Great Leader of Egypt" and a sign of the breaking of an ancient tradition in its strongest entrenchment.

The *bourgeois* home of a government official, who lives upon his salary of $50 a month, was on the third floor of an apartment building in Old Cairo. In the sitting-room of the hostess, a widow, representative of the modern type of her class, and four men were assembled to meet me. One of them, the son of the house, was a government clerk and the provider of the household. Another, a native lawyer, had evidently given deep study to the problems of Egypt.

The very intelligent conversation in this mixed group of men, women and girls, was carried on in English and

[50]

LA FEMME NOUVELLE

French, the daughter of fourteen translating into Arabic for the mother. Afternoon tea was served; certainly not a usual function, but the details were perfectly known. The dining-room was equipped with chairs, table, china, glass and napery, all the paraphernalia of modern methods, suitable for a home which was being run on a small income. The flat had bedrooms, kitchen, running water, electricity, sanitary arrangements—all of which I noticed with interest, as I had been told so often that the modern way of life was confined exclusively to the upper strata of Pashadom.

When commenting upon this in the English colony, I was met with a shrug and an "Ah, there are isolated cases, no doubt. But you should go to the Provinces." I went to the Provinces and again met these evidences of civilization, which appear in my chapters on "The Other Woman."

It was no further back than the 1870s that, in England, men broke each other's heads, shed blood and "raised Cain" generally, in order to establish universal suffrage, as it was called, though it applied to the male population only. A very large class of men, up to that time, never had been enfranchised, and it is not yet five years since suffrage has been added to the privileges of the English speaking women! Reforms take time, and "La Femme Nouvelle" goes on with her work.

There is no shop-girl class in Egypt as yet. The Moslem New Woman does not go into shops or factories. The clerks in the big foreign department stores are Copts, or foreigners; and occasionally a Coptic woman may be found as a clerk, typist, or secretary. There are a few

[51]

A WOMAN TENDERFOOT IN EGYPT

New Woman writers like Aziza Fawzy, a journalist, and Nabuwey-a-Mousa, who has written a book entitled "Women and Work." The secretary of the Ladies' Delegation, Mme. Ahmed Bey Shaker, is also a writer for the newspapers, a quiet, smiling, little woman and very efficient. She had laid aside the *habara* at an executive session where we met, and her wavy hair, parted in the middle, shone with blue and black lights. There are also a few women in the professions: Miss Sayaba is a doctor, her sister is a lawyer, and, as might be expected, the greater number of those striking out of *purdah* are teachers and nurses.

So the New Woman in Egypt, gathering strength, digs persistently at the dam of ignorance, custom and male oppression. She has become a part of the struggle for self-expression which is straining all around this spinning globe of ours. In Europe and America, in Turkey, China and Japan the woman claims a look-in, as the New Order causes Governments and social systems to totter, and fall.

In Egypt, the last representative, is the present Queen Nazli, who, by inheritance at least, is one of the progressives. Her mother was a warm friend of Mme. Zaghlul Pasha. When Her Majesty granted me an audience, which will be described in a later chapter, I was greeted by a young woman of tall, graceful beauty, who spoke most frankly about her desire for travel and liberty. Surrounded by all the pomp of an Oriental court she is watching and waiting for a weak bar in her cage of conventions, that she may snap it and push forth into a wider world.

[52]

LA FEMME NOUVELLE

If not for Her Majesty, surely for the New Woman in Egypt who has adopted Madame Zaghlul's political slogan—"We shall go on till the end"—there can be only one answer. As elsewhere, she will win the larger freedom which she seeks, not only for herself, but for her lagging sister, the Other Woman.

CHAPTER VI

PRINCESS TOSSUN AND THE YOUNGER SET

THE Princess Tossun is one of the supporters of the Mohammed Ali Society, a Moslem Woman's Organization, which also carries on many good works for the advancement of women and the alleviation of present conditions. She is an Alexandrian of noble birth and advanced ideas, and represents a considerable group of up-to-date women, whose European contact is constant, and whose cultivation and influence spread rays of inspiration downward and inspire emulation. The native press, indifferent and often hostile to the New Woman, gives no idea of what she is doing, much less thinking. The actions of the feminine population is not "news." While in Cairo, she was at the home of the Princess Hassan at Gezireh—that narrow island in the Nile where many of the fashionables of Cairo live. It is said that a member of the family, Prince Omar Tossun, was offered the Sultanate but refused, as the position promised too much British domination.

The Princess Tossun sat upon a satin sofa in the drawing-room of Mme. Riaz Pasha and conversed amiably and fluently in English on current events and upon her interest in the Mohammed Ali Society. She said that she rarely if ever wore the *boukra* but thought the dress hat was sufficient mark of respect to the old custom. This she was wearing, a confection of white tulle swirled about a round crown and held in place at intervals by large yellow roses.

The Princess and the score of other women in the room were laughing at the editorial wail in *Al Express,* in Jan. 1922, on "The New Woman in Egypt," extracts from which are here given as a sample of the publicity given to women when they are noticed. This shriek from the ancient order of things again is strongly reminiscent of the press in our own country not twenty years ago. In the parentheses are some of the comments made while this article was being read.

"A few days ago a number of Egyptian ladies of the highest society called upon the former Ministers to ask them if they proposed to accept office. These ladies were naturally without their veils, and naturally also they were dressed in the height of fashion as those who saw them told us. It seems that the Egyptian democracy induced the Ministers to meet them and to enjoy their sweet voices in order to tranquilize them on the subject and assure them that they would not accept office in order to leave the country without a native government and so spite the English and protest against their acts. ("Disgusting.")

"When these ladies had taken coffee and refreshment they left, and we wonder if they were dismissed with the usual courtesies. ("Most insulting.") What we know, however, is that if the late Riaz Pasha rose from the dead and saw the conduct of the Egyptian woman, how she meets men, with or without the consent of her husband, he would prefer to go back to eternal life and abandon this world in which oriental Moslem habits and character have reached such a point. ("Nonsense," said the widow of Riaz Pasha.)

"An Egyptian lady meets a man who is not her husband, tears her veil and treads on the habits and traditions of her nation! What great success! What wonderful advancement! What tremendous change! The late Kassem Amin Bey was attacked not because he recommended that the veil should be done away with, but because he recommended that the girl should be educated. ("How men hate to have us think!")

"We have also noticed that ladies and young ladies sign protests with their names, when the man used to be ashamed to give the name of his wife or daughter in official documents of sale or purchase. What a great change in the short space of a few years! ("Yes, indeed, Praise Allah!")

"The Egyptian lady has not only protested, but also interfered in the matter of boycottage. ("We certainly have!") We are in need of their patriotism—not by words, but by acts—to boycott English goods till they find the same articles manufactured by other countries, for the Egyptian woman is the greatest consumer of English goods, particularly the most expensive. ("A lie! None of us are buying English goods.")

During this conversation, which might have occurred in any drawing-room of the upper class in any European nation, I heard "through an open door" strains of last year's jazz music. A group of a dozen of the younger set had collected in the music-room where the tea-table was placed. They were all in French clothes with a tendency to bright colors and heavy velvets. They all spoke Arabic and French, and most of them Italian and English. They do charity and club work, and even dabble in

THE YOUNGER SET

politics. They gossip and go to the movies. They ride
and play tennis. They bathe in the sea and go picnick-
ing. They dance and flirt with each other's younger
brothers and cousins. Male relatives are admitted
to home festivities, and the matter of blood relation-
ship is becoming more elastic from a social standpoint.

I remember another picture which this younger set of
moderns and their friends, made in the great hall of the
palace of Mme. Omar Sultan Pasha. A small orchestra
provided the music, and the smartly-gowned girls, dancing
with boys and a few older men relatives, or with each
other, jazzed away the afternoon most merrily. A lavish
buffet with a profusion of fancy sandwiches, cakes and
soft drinks, was spread in the palatial dining-room and a
host of women and some men drifted through the richly-
furnished drawing-rooms. I was not made conscious of
their restricted lives, and certainly the women I met do
not worry over it. On one occasion I asked a group of
these young Moslem women to tea in a public restaurant
and was told that they preferred not to go often to public
places so long as they were wearing the *habara* because it
attracted so much attention that they were made uncomfortable. One of them remarked, "It will not last much
longer."

The crowning beauty in this country of beautiful
women, and good example of the younger set, is Mlle.
Sennia Riaz Pasha, here shown in Circassian costume.
The amateur photographer has done his best to destroy
the luscious Oriental charm of this daughter of the land
of Cleopatra—the creamy skin, and languorous, yet intelligent, dark eyes that look at one through heavy lashes,

[57]

which have been liberally touched with kohl, thereby extending the almond shape of the eyes, even as depicted in the tomb paintings of Egyptian queens, 4,000 years ago. This gorgeous young woman belongs to a wealthy and powerful family and is active in the exclusive Cairean society, but finds plenty of time to do club and welfare work and even to assist in the dangerous political manifestations which the women have organized in the last two years. She is engaged to be married to a cousin, whom, in accordance with the modern custom, she has often seen. She wears very smart French frocks and the thinnest of veils. In a public place—it was at an exhibition of native industries, very beautiful products of the manufacturers of cotton, silk, leather, wood, brass, and even plumbing and phonograph articles—I noticed that Mlle. Sennia had dropped her veil. I remarked upon this. "Oh, there are no men of importance here and we don't bother about servants." This lovely vision, who combines intelligence and cultivation with her beauty, assured me that when she married she would keep her property under her control. She also told me the following facts about the laws regarding women and children:

"When a man of the middle or lower class takes a wife he pays her father so much for being deprived of her services and if he divorces the woman she goes back to her father with one and a half that sum again, 'in payment for the pleasure and profit the man has had.'

"A Moslem girl rarely sees her betrothed before marriage. The match is arranged by her parents. Therefore, the principal contracting parties may find serious inharmonies,

[58]

though the easy divorce makes this bearable; but it is often kinder for a man to take a second wife than to divorce his first, thereby depriving her of his financial support.

"If she is wealthy, there are the marriage settlements by which the property remains under the exclusive control of the woman, whether as wife, or divorced. This is a Mohammedan law."

Other laws not unfavourable to women are: In the event of divorce the children may remain with the mother, or mother's mother, until, in case of a boy, the age of 7, or of a girl, the age of 9, when the law allows the father to claim them; unless he has married again and has children, in which case the maternal grandmother gets them.

Mlle. Sennia Riaz Pasha discussed sex and marriage with all the freedom of a young college woman of America. Her ideas agreed with those of the *Sub Mudir*, the Assistant Governor of one of the principal Nile Provinces, who told me that, "While it is true that our religion permits four wives, no man can now take a second wife without justifying his action to himself and to his friends. It is against public opinion. And Mohammed in making four wives legal did not order that it should be so, but permitted a man to marry up to that number in order to stop immorality and promiscuity. European men have their mistresses. The Moslem takes another wife. Is it really any different except that the Moslem is franker about it?

"There are four conditions under which a man is justified in taking a second wife.

"The first is incompatibility of temperament. The second, presumed sterility of the first wife. The third, the possession of some disease dangerous to public or family health, such as consumption or venereal disease. The fourth is that the first wife does not satisfy her husband in the marital relation. This reason is rarely accepted nowadays as a cause for divorce."

CHAPTER VII

NAZLI: QUEEN OF EGYPT

A ROYAL CAPTIVE

A CONSPICUOUS example of the Gilded-Cage Fraternity today is Her Majesty the Queen of Egypt.

This is the more marked in that the lady herself, Queen Nazli, who is young and very beautiful, is of the modern spirit and fully realizes her clipped wings. Her Majesty granted me a glimpse into the magnificent isolation of her estate at Abdin Palace, Cairo, in the spring of 1922, when Egypt was changing into a Kingdom and Lord Allenby was accomplishing his mission of mediation with the British Foreign Office for a further move in the game of Egypt's independence.

A few further high lights of "restless Egypt" and of its King must be noted down, in order to understand the background of this Royal Consort, and the paradox of an Oriental Queen as a "New Woman."

The Sultan, Ahmed Fuad Pasha, was made King of Egypt on March 16, 1922, by a British proclamation making Egypt a "Sovereign, Independent State." This left several causes of trouble still to be dealt with, such as the changing authority between the British civil administration and the Egyptian government; the protection of European interests and residents; and the future status of the Sudan. The inevitable friction of adjustment has

[61]

been greatly increased by the Zaghlulists, who use every opportunity to stir up the Egyptians against the British in the hope of obtaining control of "Egypt for the Egyptians." The results are riots, bloodshed, reprisals and endless disturbances, in a situation which, in itself, is difficult. Verily, "uneasy lies the head that wears a crown."

The "New Woman" movement whose roots have spread into Egypt, as related in preceding chapters, must be remembered as an outstanding feature in the background of Egypt's Queen. It has had a definite effect upon her character, for Queen Nazli by inheritance belongs to the "New Woman" group, her mother having been a close friend of Mme. Zaghlul Pasha and other Progressives.

Many of these modern, high-born, women do not attend the Queen's receptions, in consequence of a belief that her royal Husband favours the British rather than the Egyptians.

My interview with the Queen revealed a woman whose spirit is free and who will take advantage of every opportunity offered her to break down the barriers of custom that surround the Moslem woman. One observes with interest the greater liberty allowed Fewkie, daughter of King Fuad by a former marriage, and wife of Mahmound Pasha Fachry. The Princess Fewkie, who is about the same age as the Queen, has possessed herself of much liberty for a Mohammedan woman; she goes to Europe when she wishes and, with an equal show of independence, has appeared on occasions in public, even in Egypt, without her "veil." The difference between the kingly sanction of freedom of action between daughter and wife is elsewhere explained under the heading of jealousy—which to the Oriental mind still appears more of a virtue than a vice.

The most important figure that looms in Nazli's background, and the only man outside of her immediate relatives, is her Royal Spouse. The routine of King Fuad's day, as outlined by one close to him, is as follows: After a late breakfast, state papers are brought to him by his Minister for approval and signature or veto. Any measures calculated to improve the condition of his people command his kindly interest. During the morning he receives distinguished visitors. He lunches at about half-past one, usually with men guests invited through the Court Chamberlain. Before his accession King Fuad spent most of his time in Italy leading the life of a scion of a royal line without a throne, but with much money and small ambition. But several prominent Americans to whom he has given audiences recently have been impressed by his progressive spirit, his desire for more widespread education and development of business interests, for a freer press and establishment of American banks and American investment generally. After luncheon he indulges in the siesta common to hot countries. He dines about eight with the Queen. He is past fifty, of somewhat corpulent figure and of medium height. King Fuad has a superstition that the letter F is lucky for him. All of his children's names begin with it.

Nazli, born in 1899, was a girl of eighteen when she received the news that a marriage had been arranged with Ahmed Fuad Pasha who had recently been made Sultan. It must be recorded that there were tearful ob-

jections, mixed with gratified pride—for the daughter of
Abdurachman Pasha Sabry, while of excellent family, is
not of royal descent. She had travelled abroad and
mixed with the modern women in Egypt and the thirst
for freedom had begun its work. She did not want to
sacrifice her young life to a stout, oldish man, and her
liberty to a ruler who does not live in the hearts of his
people.

However, the discipline of the Egyptian family of
Turkish descent is founded on parental respect and the
wedding of Nazli was soon a *"fait accompli."* There
was no blaze of trumpets. The Sultan thought it unwise
to risk his person before his people. Three years ago
Egypt was very turbulent as indeed it still is. Only the
members and friends of the immediate families were present with two ladies-in-waiting in attendance on the young
bride.

Madame Joseph Aslau Cattaui Pasha was one of these
attendants and is today the Lady Chamberlain. She is
a very beautiful woman: Snow-white hair elegantly
dressed, framing a young fair-skinned face of cameo
outlines, a pure profile, aquiline nose—brilliant eyes,
not dark, and a slim elegant figure. This Egyptian
lady dresses in smart French frocks, and speaks many
languages in a soft, rich voice.

However much the King, in the past, through fear or
policy, may have chosen to withdraw himself from the
public, the captivity of the Queen is involuntary. To
be sure, she does visit her parents and she does travel
every summer from Abdin Palace to her palace on the
seashore at Alexandria which "is so very damp." And
there she remains during the heated term until it is time

to exchange her gilded cage for another gorgeous prison.

I was told that the Queen had "much liberty" and could "receive whom she likes." This proved to be a play on words. When I asked if Her Majesty went out, I was told—"Ah, no, of course she does not go out of the palace." I also heard that "receiving whom one liked" consists in submitting a list of *ladies only* to Her Majesty's Chamberlain, who censors it and submits it to the King who approves as many names as he wishes —a royal fit of indigestion might easily rob the Queen's audience-chamber of visitors.

Audience with royalty is often no more difficult to obtain than an interview with one of our local industrial or financial kings, a Morgan or a Rockefeller. One must have a friend at court and a convincing reason for desiring to intrude upon the person in question. In the case of the Queen of Egypt who "rarely receives foreigners," it was more complicated and the ceremony more elaborate. The preliminaries were arranged by Lady Congreve, wife of the British Commander-in-Chief, who called one evening at six o'clock and took the ladies who wished to be received to Abdin Palace for the signature ceremony. This meant going to the palace in person to "write our names in the book" and afterwards the sending of several visiting cards to the Chamberlain, through our sponsors.

General Congreve's motor was driven by a uniformed British soldier and a dark flunky in Egyptian costume of red, embroidered in gold, balloon trousers, Zouave jacket and a *tarbush*. Each gate of the various courts of the Palace was guarded by soldiers. The Queen's palace stands in a court which is formed by the hollow

[65]

square of the King's palace. We passed a line of ten soldiers in Egyptian costume at the entrance of the inner court. All saluted.

Then the gilded wrought-iron gates of the Queen's palace were opened by a eunuch and closed upon us. Inside, at the foot of a most imposing stairway, stood three women. One, dressed in dark striped blue velvet, of European cut, upon her ample person, seemed the superior. Another was in black velveteen with a large rose embroidered in gold; on the left breast she wore a turban of gold and pink roses, and was evidently a palace attendant. The third woman, hovering in the background, was in pink calico; an overgarment of white lace, coarse and of cotton, draped her head and the upper part of the body. She was middle-aged and smiling and ample and might easily have been a child's nurse. The lady in blue velvet wore nothing upon her abundant black hair. With a smile in lieu of speech, she motioned us to a marble and gilt table upon which was "the book" in which the names of all visitors must be written. She extended to me a silver penholder. Two other silver penholders were upon a silver tray near the massive silver ink-well.

A gold basket of gold-coloured roses was on the table and one on each of the consoles with which the large room was furnished. The reception room was very spacious, situated at the top of a truly palatial grand stairway of marble which had royal crimson rugs spread on four feet of the centre of it; its ceiling reached into the shadows.

The Queen was receiving perhaps a dozen visitors, if one could judge by the wraps left in the outer hall through which we now passed. It was fully 70 feet wide. The great gilded doors opened and shut. A scurry of polite but formidable creatures in gorgeous gold and red tunics and yellow trousers, and carrying huge scimitars in their sashes, produced our motor and our departure was accomplished.

The audience was finally arranged about a month later, on February 21, 1922, through the American Minister, Dr. J. Morton Howell, and again our party was negotiating the imposing entrance of Abdin Palace, this time under the wing of Mrs. Howell.

Passing through the inner court of Queen Nazli's palace we arrived at a beautiful doorway of iron and gold. Two eunuchs in gorgeous gold-embroidered liveries stood outside. Within were a dozen women attendants, dressed in velvet of different colours. One was gold, another brown, another bright blue, another maroon, the skirts were full and trailing, the basques were simple in cut with long sleeves and the plump uncorseted figures were all caught in at the waist by a narrow belt. This produced a mid-Victorian silhouette not beautiful according to present notions of the female figure. But the lady-in-waiting who received us at the top of the grand stairway was quite another matter, the same distinguished, *chic* and beautiful person I had seen before. It was the Lady Chamberlain, Madame Joseph Aslan Cattaui Pasha. Her gown was French, grey chiffon and silver lace, worn with elegance and charm. She initiated us into the mysteries of a first audience with such tact that one was hardly conscious of direction.

In excellent English she told us of the little two-year-old prince, Farouk, and the baby Princess Fatchuya, and showed us a portrait of King Fuad I. She conducted us through splendid drawing-rooms furnished formally in the French style, heavy brocades and satins and walnut, and panelled in gilt, with several deep-seated divans where an Oriental could, if so inclined, indulge in the fast-disappearing habit of sitting cross-legged. The only personal touch in these formal rooms were the exquisite flowers.

Then we passed a line of the gold, blue, purple and brown velveted females and entered the audience chamber, a very big apartment, as we realized when the time came to back out of it. The American Minister's wife headed the procession of five as we advanced Indian file and in turn gave the salute. This consisted of touching the tips of the Queen's fingers and dropping to the ground, or as near it as one could manage, in a courtesy; the thoroughly-American, no longer young, nor slim, matron in front of me contented herself with a very slight obeisance, but atoned for it by saying:

"I do not wonder that your husband does not want to allow you out without a veil."

Her Majesty laughed a fresh, rather high-pitched, peal and the ice was broken.

"Ah, Madame, but you must not say that to the King, you must say I am perfectly safe to go out alone, for he is very jealous. He says he will not allow the new telephone in the palace, the one which shows you the person who is speaking. It is terrible, he is very jealous."

The voice, however, betrayed but little emotion. There was nothing tragic about her. This slim and beautiful woman of 22 knows her fate and has accepted it.

NAZLI: QUEEN OF EGYPT

She enjoys her children, her jewels, her women friends and the gorgeous setting of her restricted life.

The Queen seated herself upon a brown satin sofa at the end of the room. It was fully eight feet long. Armchairs, similarly upholstered, were ranged at right-angles on either side. In these we were seated, the most important personage being nearest the Queen. Over her head was a life-sized portrait of the grandfather-in-law, the Khedive Ismail.

Her Majesty wore dark green velvet and gold, a Paris creation. Several very large diamonds were upon her slender fingers and an enormous diamond, the size of a small walnut, dangled by long platinum chains from each ear. The gems quivered and sparkled like live things. Her hair was done in the latest French twist, with a large tortoiseshell comb, placed low, Spanish fashion. Her skin was fair: eyes and lips much made up, after the Oriental mode, which seems to suit these beauties of Egypt. She is simple and charming. She seemed like a rare jewel hidden away in a gorgeous cabinet.

Masses of Malmaison carnations of unusual size were arranged formally in silver bowls on each side of the satin sofa. There were roses in rare glass vases, marvellous roses, red on this day but never the same colour on two consecutive days. On my first visit, they were all *Marechal Niel* and tea roses.

I spoke to the young Queen of the growing freedom of women in Egypt.

"Yes, it is coming,—but slowly. I hope my little girl may be able to travel and go about. For me it is still difficult." I remembered that the Queen never leaves the palace. The face clouded, but again cleared determinedly. "I have told the King that when he travels he must take me with him. I do not want to be left here. But I do not know that he will. He is very jealous.

"I have not been to Europe since I was thirteen. You know the Moslem girls are veiled at fourteen, and then, I was so young and I had so much family always about me. I have two sisters and several brothers. It was hard to understand much of what I was seeing. I was seventeen before I began to learn English and I speak French much better, and Italian and Arabic of course."

The Queen's next remark was significant, "Indeed I would like to go to America. It must be a wonderful country. I have told the King that the next time he travels I want to go with him." She repeated the wish evidently so dear to her heart. "I do not want to stay here all the time. In summer I go to Alexandria but it is very damp there. I want to go to Europe. But the King is very jealous." (An arch little smile.) "It is terrible and so foolish."

"The women are becoming much more free," I said. "You know the organization of 'La Femme Nouvelle' and what they are trying to do?"

"Oh, yes, I know something of it. They are wonderful, those women. I may not get it—but—I hope that my little Fatchuya will have more freedom."

I asked permission to send her an English book which she granted. "I shall be most happy to have it. It is hard to get good English books here. I shall read it for myself and soon I can read it to little Farouk. He is beginning to speak English now." (At the age of two!) "Send the book to Madame Cattaui Pasha for me and she will see that I get it." Apparently even a little matter of a book from a woman had to be censored.

At the end of half an hour, cakes and coffee were served, the coffee a thick Oriental concoction in small silver filagree cups. These were passed to us in order of dignity—the question of rank amongst Americans often is an awkward one for the Chamberlain. And after this ceremony, in which the Queen did not participate, she gave the signal for dismissal by rising, my democratic neighbour having previously tried to rise and having been nodded down by our sponsor who knew the custom of royalty. We again bent our respective knees and courtesied over the Royal hand.

Thus we leave her, the young Nazli of Egypt, surrounded by exotic flowers with the great portrait of the Khedive Ismail as a background, standing like the Queen she is, in all her slim elegance and modern attire, graciously acknowledging our salutes as we backed out of her presence. The last thing I saw, as I democratically waved my hand to her, now fully sixty feet away, was a white hand making a like response causing the large diamonds upon her fingers and others equally resplendent in her ears to flash like signals of light in a rich, but dark, setting.

BOOK I

PART II

FATIMA AS SHE IS TODAY

II

THE OTHER WOMAN AND HER
EDUCATION

CHAPTER VIII

THE FELLAHEEN

EGYPT, of all lands today, is a country of paradoxes, of sharp contrasts and of silhouettes. Already we have seen the New Woman in her ultra-modernity. Like lightning in a darkened sky she streaks through the mass of Egyptian womanhood—the Other Woman—who is found among the varying grades of *fellaheen,* or peasants, of the Bedouins, and the lower *bourgeoisie.* Even as yeast gives life to the freshly mixed dough, so the changing values and conditions of social and economic life are permeating to the lowest stratum of the dwellers of the Blue Nile. The yeast, as elsewhere, is education and opportunity. We have seen how the thinking Egyptian man and woman wants to take a place on the international merry-go-round, and before we consider the condition upon which they are working, it may be interesting to give some of the statements advanced against this desire, from the British point of view. Firstly, the Egyptians are incapable of governing themselves, the mass of the people, the *fellaheen,* are much happier than they have ever been, and they want no change of government. Their rights are protected under the British police-court system and the "five-feddans law," established by Lord Kitchener, which keeps them out of absolute want. Secondly, that the Egyptian, in fact any Oriental, mind is not basically

[75]

honest: that although he may not steal, he is not above twisting facts to suit his purpose, and that intrigues of the ruling classes and oppression by them of the lower classes would soon ruin the country. Thirdly, that the Egyptian is essentially an agriculturist, not a trader, not a fighter, not an administrator; that the trade is now largely in the hands of the ubiquitous Greek. Therefore, as now, the Italian, French and English will control the manufactures and such staple products as cotton and sugar. Fourthly, that the Desert Arabs and Upper Nile warlike tribes would harass and even terrorize the people, and that no government which the Egyptians might form "would be wise enough to work out a national unity."

Many of these arguments remind one of the recent days when the fight was on for woman's suffrage and indeed, not so long ago, for male suffrage. It is the world-wide struggle of the under-dog to reverse his position. At any rate, it is apparent that Egypt's will to know and to govern herself has resulted in England's giving her the opportunity to do so, and the rest is on the knees of the Gods.

Now let us return to the banks of the River-that-Flows-up-Stream—where Modern Egypt, including the New Woman, is eclipsed in its past.

The Great Pyramids of Gizeh and that strange figure, the Sphinx, cut out sharply against the sky, call to one from the ages, reaching back into the unheralded past. They dominate on the west, miles of desert, which stretch away into the sunset, unchanged and unchanging. On the east, the Sun-God Ra still sweeps his chariot over fertile fields, active little villages and a network of canals,

[76]

where the life of the *fellaheen* is lived in careless, even happy, disregard for the comforts of a modern life.

These workers of the soil represent about two-thirds of Egypt's population. They are ignorant, illiterate, but happy and smiling. They are hard-working and home-loving. The women are trained to carry loads upon the head. This gives them a beautiful carriage and a sure tread.

At sundown the women make a picturesque sight going to the river, or canal, to fill the family water *ghoula,* their black garments trailing in long lines from head to foot. The water hour is the "five o'clock tea" for them, the *fellah* Woman's Club. They gossip and chatter and bathe their feet and, often, wash their dresses. The news of their little world, and scraps from the great world, are bandied about. Their faces are rarely sad. They cannot read and are superstitiously dominated by the priests, be they Mohammedan or Copt (Christian). Their ideas about sanitation and hygiene are as hazy as the fear of our modern bug-a-boo, the germ. No nightmares for them of odd-shaped creatures, wriggling on a glass plate —a thousand times magnified so that we may have a proper respect for them. Until education fills the bitter-sweet twin cups of knowledge, these women will accept the hard conditions of their lives, much as the animals do.

Indeed, the first thing that impressed me was that the *fallaheen* family seems to have divided a small Noah's ark with its neighbour. A child, woman or old man will be seen guarding a group of animals whose types have not changed since Joseph's time, nor Pharaoh's time, nor from the time of the first dynasty kings, well-nigh seven thousand years ago. There will be a water buffalo, a donkey, a goat and a brown woolly sheep grazing upon a patch of clover, or pulse, grown for their benefit. The Egyptian animal is an intensive eater, perforce, guided by its shepherd. Only so many square feet a day may be eaten, and the patch is left with roots intact to recover in three months' time for another meal. Verily, as in Bible times, the lower-class *fellaheen* family and its animals lie down together in the mud-walled enclosure, called home. After the human small fry take nourishment from the goat, they snuggle for warmth against the soft brown wool of the sheep. The simplicity of the domestic arrangements is so foreign to our highy-developed needs, that, until one can get the animal's point of view, one cannot understand how these children of the soil can manage. Their houses seldom have roofs, perhaps a shade of straw matting over one part of the enclosure to temper the sun. There are no floors, no furniture, no water and no sanitary arrangements. No provision for storing belongings, other than a few holes in the wall. There is nothing to store.

A small brazier, a handful of bean-flour, a porous water-jar filled from the river every evening, and a half-dozen copper, or earthern, pots, constituted the entire equipment of a house I inspected near the Tomb of the Kings at Luxor last February. It was built on a slope of the desert without a tree, or a green leaf, in sight. Slipping off our donkeys, I waited while Shehata, my dragoman, knocked at a wooden door, set in a rough wall. Nobody was at home but the goat. Immediately the deserted place swarmed with children apparently coming from nowhere. A woman, the owner, carrying a baby, straddle-wise on her hip, appeared from a distant house and bade me enter.

This home consisted of four enclosures, each one on a different level. Two of them roughly roofed over with poles of uneven lengths, had chaff sugar-cane laid upon them and weighted with stones against the desert winds. The walls were about six feet high and six inches thick, rudely built of mud and straw with uneven tops forming irregular enclosures where the cattle, sheep and humans all lived together. An oven of baked mud and a water receptacle, like a large shallow basin, and several pots and shallow dishes, all of baked mud, comprised the entire furniture.

The floor was the desert sand, mixed with animal and human litter. There were no beds, tables, chairs—not even a mat for the family to sleep upon. They simply curled up on the filthy ground, often against the sheep, and endured the flies and fleas with equal indifference.

They had no clothing but the black rags on their backs. The small boys were naked. One brown garment, an *abayeh*, of coarse woollen weave, doubtless plucked from the back of their sheep, twisted into a rope by means of a spindle, and woven on a handloom, was the family's sole additional garment. It hung over the low wall that partially divided the interior space, one portion of which was evidently intended for the animals, as the floor was full of drying manure which is baked and used for fertilizer. A small earthen pot contained some coarse yellow meal which would be mixed with hot water and, first, sunbaked, perhaps, then placed in an oven afterwards,

[79]

A WOMAN TENDERFOOT IN EGYPT

It was the only visible food, and the bowl was covered by a larger one and again by a still larger heavy one to keep the sheep and cow out of it.

The mistress of the home, with four children and her husband, got along on this. She was 25, looked 40, and said she was the only wife of her husband. Doubtless somewhere, tucked away in a hole, was a gold ornament or two that the woman put on for gala occasions. There is little else to tell about her. She goes daily to the River for water, once a week into market for supplies. She does her simple tasks, gossips with her neighbours, and sees the priest on fête days. Her husband, besides his four animals and some chickens, undoubtedly had his five *feddans* of land which he tills or rents to others. The family seemed happy and healthy, and no dirtier than the animals with which they live, while their animal needs are satisfied as simply. But there is one colossal difference between the lamb running by its mother's side and the smiling beady-eyed boy clutching at his mother's skirt, the power of intellect. The one will never be anything but a sheep, the other may be the creator of his country's greatness. A few years from now, the lamb will be represented only by its progeny, the boy may know Arabic, perhaps French, and English. He will know the Koran, arithmetic, elementary economics and a mass of information, good, bad and indifferent, which will enable him to till his fields, or, it may be, to take a Government position, or even to become a lawyer, a doctor, or a leader among men. Thus wondrous is the way of human consciousness. There is a Rosicrucian diagram of man's place in the universe. It shows two triangles, one inverted and placed upon the other, the points meeting.

[80]

THE FELLAHEEN

The bottom triangle represented the animal and lower consciousness from which man had sprung; the upper the spiritual consciousness towards which man aspires. At the junction of the two points is man, contacting the lower consciousness, capable of contacting the spiritual. What a man chooseth to be, that is he.

CHAPTER IX

THE RICH PEASANT

LORD CROMER organized many reforms for Egypt, including the irrigation regulations so that all farmers might get their fair share of water, but the crowning achievement for the peasant was Lord Kitchener's five-feddans law, of which mention has already been made. This provides for the continued possession of that much land, (approximately five acres), by a *fellah,* whether he will or not. He has no power to sell or mortgage his last five feddans. He cannot give them away. They are not seizable for debt. They are his, and his children's after him. Gradually the industrious peasant has acquired more and more fields "next to his'n," until many of these hard-working steady sons and daughters of the soil have become rich. The price of cotton has greatly advanced, as high as £40 the bale in 1919. The steady crops of sugar cane, wheat and barley and alfalfa and beans feed him and his animals. His wants are few. He has grown richer, until an income of $75,000 a year is not a miracle and yearly incomes of $40,000 to $50,000 are not uncommon.

An example of these rich peasant women, Sitt Gaba, I met amongst the group in Mme. Zaghlul Pasha's drawing-room and described in the dealing with "Madame Zaghlul Pasha and The Ladies' Wafd."

After the rich peasant woman has loaded down her

THE RICH PEASANT

person with solid gold ornaments, her ambition is satisfied. She provides liberally for the family table, and still the money pours in. She banks it, and the interest soon begins to compound. An increasing percentage of the growing generation want education. They want to spend the money which takes them into the big cities, and here they soon realize the need for knowledge. They are out from under the rule of the local priest. The children of these emancipated ones are most certainly sent to a good school, and the young men become recruits into the government official, or the professional, classes, and a sprinkling of the girls also push out into the larger world. One reason why the peasants love Saad Zaghlul Pasha so much and offered their weath so freely for him to spend in the struggle for Egypt's independence, is because he was one of them and, by dint of hard work and ability, raised himself to his present high estate.

CHAPTER X

THE BEDOUIN

THE Bedouins must not be confused with the *fellaheen.* They consider themselves much superior and, even towards the upper classes, they hold themselves as "different," not inferior. They are the Princes of the Desert, a free race, bowing the knee to no outside ruler, and even have certain privileges in their allegiance to Egypt. The Bedouin is exempt from police or military duty. Being of brave and fearless spirit, however, he often volunteers for fighting; and organized revolts against the Government are not unknown. The last one occurred during the Great War, among the Senussi, a tribe of fanatical Moslems.

The Bedouins live in villages on the edge of the desert, on oases, and in travelling tent-caravans which camp in the desert wherever water can be obtained and "pull up stakes," to use the Western vernacular, when the restless nomadic spirit seizes them. The Sheikh, partly hereditary, and partly elective, is the ruler over the Bedouin tribes. A Sheikh of Sheikhs is called an Emdeh. They are Mohammedans, and practise the tenets of their faith religiously under the sway of the Ulima, or priest.

The Bedouin men that I have met had fine physiques, were very intelligent and honest and polite. They were clannish, taking good care of their families and relatives.

THE BEDOUIN

I saw no beggars amongst them. The position of the
women is not high, owing to the Moslem restriction on
female education, but this is slowly breaking down. The
Bedouin women are well cared for, never maltreated, so
far as I could discover, and have an affectionate family
life. Those I knew were tall and graceful and mentally
alert.

SHEHATA'S HOME

My delightful woman companion on these desert trips
was the Poet, and one afternoon in February we set forth
on camels for an hour's ride from Meneh House to visit
the two homes of our Bedouin dragoman, Shehata Abou
Taleb, who lives at Kefia about five miles south of the
Great Pyramids. It was four o'clock and the sun was beginning to lessen its heat. We threaded our way on the
edge of the desert through the fertile alfalfa fields of the
Nile belt, through native and mud-brick villages, and
nearing Shehata's home, on the way from one village to
another, we met one of his nieces, Hamida, age 15, married and carrying a first-born. She was a handsome girl
with the usual luscious eyes and clear skin. She wished
"the Ladies all Happiness," and made the characteristic
salute of respect, touching the forehead lightly with the
finger.

Shehata's cousin, the Sheikh Mohammed, is an Emdeh.
He rules over five villages with 8,000 Bedouins and has
for wife, Sitt Elia, a very good-looking woman of 28, with
light skin and refined features. She, with a pretty
daughter of eight, was waiting to receive us at the home
of Shehata's second wife, Margliyeh, aged 22, who was
about to produce her first-born. We were ushered into a

small reception room, built on the right of a scattered group of buildings, enclosed in a high stucco wall, parts of which formed the outside wall of the rooms. In the reception room, shabby upholstered settees were on two sides. One was covered with white linen, and we made for that. A cheap rug was on the stone floor, and a dilapidated table, on which stood a rough make-shift for a tea-service, arranged for our benefit, with crockery and pewter spoons.

Shehata had excused himself earlier in the day and travelled all the way into Cairo from the Meneh House, an hour each way by tram, in order to buy the tea, cream, seeded cakes and fresh butter which were now offered to us. These delicacies had been sent ahead to his village by a friendly Bedouin, and with true courtesy, nothing was said about the effort to give us the "English Tea."

The Bedouin women do not smoke tobacco, nor do they eat with the men, as a rule. Of the three native women present, the visiting wife of the Emdeh accepted tea after we had been served, as did also her daughter; likewise Shehata and his little favourite son, Samiel. The new young second wife, Margliyeh, either from disinclination or inhibitive custom, refused to eat. She preferred to turn the battery of her attention upon my person, which she did with great detail and frankness.

She looked at my string of pearls and remarked that they might be much longer, then at my gold watch and wrist band and asked why it was not made of diamonds. I showed her the three diamond rings on my fingers, hoping to make a favourable impression. She

[86]

remarked that the stones were not big enough and my fingers should be covered with them. She scrutinized the Poet and questioned:

"This is your sister? You do not look alike. You are younger than I expected. You are very pretty."

This was better, and I hoped against facts that she was being as frank now as in her previous remarks. I gave her a gold coin of Uncle Sam's Mint, and she was pleased. All Arabs love the shining gold metal. She wished me "long life and a good stomach," the Arab salutation of politeness.

I asked Margliyeh if she would like to go to America.

"Yes, but in one of the big ships of the air. I would like to fly through the sky like the birds." She promised to be sure to educate her first-born, whether it proved to be boy or girl.

"It is bad for women to know nothing. Yes, yes, it shall be done." By request, she then took me to see her bedroom, which was one of a series of rooms built around an open enclosure of the desert sand, perhaps 200 yards square. No attempt had been made to beautify the court-yard, and the livestock of the several families of relatives who dwelt therein, was all herded in it each night, not the only primitive touch one sees in the Bedouin village.

Margliyeh's room had three solid walls. The fourth on the open court was pierced by the door and a window which was fitted with glass and shutters and cretonne drapery. The bed of iron and brass, with springs, mattress, pillows, sheets and comforters, was modern, and canopied with the same cretonne as the window A wooden bureau with a mirror over it, a six-foot divan which could also be slept upon, a row of cushioned seats on the floor against the wall, fresh straw matting and a rack on the wall for clothes, comprised the furnishings of this not really typical room. The bed, especially, showed the European influence, as the Bedouin, like the native low-class town-dweller, can sleep anywhere. With a piece of matting or quilt under him, he curls up in his garments with the head, and usually the face, well covered, and slips off into the borderland of angels or devils with more ease, perhaps, than our pampered cushioned bodies can achieve.

Shehata's first wife, also named Elia, whom I had not met before, greeted me with many salutations and smiles. She is now 38, has six children, five sons and one daughter, Mansourah, who is already engaged. Ten years ago, when Mansourah was five, Shehata had promised me that she should be educated in the same manner as his sons. He had kept his word until a year ago, when he had a command from the Ulima to withdraw Mansourah from school as he did not approve of the higher education of women. It unfits them for the life of subjection to priest and man. Shehata was distressed, as the Bedouin does not lightly forget a vow, neither does he lightly disobey the command of a Mohammedan Priest. He solved the problem to his satisfaction by betrothing her to a very eligible youth, a son of his cousin, the big Sheikh Mahmoud. This Moslem religious opposition to higher education springs from the fact that the language of literature is distinct from the dialect which the *fellaheen* and lower classes speak, and from the affinity of this written language to that of the Koran.   But even so, this opposition is being broken down as the higher school statistics show.

Shehata seemed on very good terms with the still handsome Elia, whom he divorced for the same reason as the negro wench in Tennessee, who said, when asked why she wanted to divorce Sambo, "Well, you see, Jedge, I jes' naturally got tired of the man."   Shehata continues to support Elia and her home, which he frequently visits. He loves their children, kisses them affectionately many times.   They are well-cared for and well-clothed, and often go with him in his second home, especially the little seven-year-old favourite, Samiel; but Elia never goes.   She lives in a comfortable three-story house, not half a mile away, with other related families, and seems quite happy, though, with a smiling face she said, "Is it not a shame that Shehata should take another wife when he has such a big family here?   But he is very good to me," she added, "and to the children."   I regretted that my limited Arabic made it difficult to get at the psychology of this.   Elia was a mixture of resignation, bitterness, jealousy and indifference, and even contentment, over her divorced state, which produced apparently a not-unhappy woman.   Her attitude seemed similar to that of the third wife of a Mormon who once made a trenchant remark to me when I asked her if she liked sharing her husband.   "Sharing him!   That is the beauty of it.   I do not have to.   Unless you are unfortunate enough to be the *favourite* wife, you can have your own home, enjoy your own children, lead your own life and you do not have to be bothered with a man around all the time."

A WOMAN TENDERFOOT IN EGYPT

SITT ABOUKA'S HOME

Among the Bedouins who have come to live in the town and are merging into the *bourgeoisie* I had an excellent example in the home of Sitt Abouka, the wife of a prosperous dragoman in the centre of the city of Luxor. The title *Sitt* in a measure corresponds to Mrs. or Miss. It is a term of respect used for the Arabian woman of the people, just as the title *hanem* means lady of gentle birth.

I was projected into Abdul Galeel's house unexpectedly, and therefore saw it off guard, about ten o'clock at night. Although I did not realize it until too late, this was a breach of courtesy as it would have been with us. Shehata had taken advantage of his friendship with the master of the house. Sitt Abouka, aroused from her slumbers, proved to be very amiable about it, and as the custom is to remove but the day garment for the night garment, there was only a moment's delay before she was ready. She opened the door and partly veiled herself with her head-covering when she saw Shehata, although he was visiting in the house. We were admitted to a very respectable three-story stucco house with iron balconies. It was somewhat of a shock to stumble upon the goat in the front hall. The reason for it was soon obvious. The hall was paved with red tiles back as far as the staircase only. Beyond that, the bare ground served, and the rear room was developed into a stable from where a loud-voiced donkey brayed, and a water-buffalo grunted. No doubt the woolly sheep was there too, and the goat had her place. Some chickens strayed

[90]

about. On the railing of the second landing which was open to the weather, roosted three turkeys! The Bedouin is accustomed to do his own policing out on the desert, and the best way to take care of property is to have it under one's eye. Hence the St. Francis of Assisi effect in this house.

There was a row of settees that also served for beds in the reception room on the right of the entrance, and a large utility room on the left. My hostess soon led me to the second story, leaving Shehata downstairs. We entered a large bedroom. It had several pegs on the wall where hung the gorgeous robes which her husband the guide wears, a chest of drawers, red-tiled floor and three single beds ranged along the wall. They had mattresses and some tossed-about comforters, but no sheets.

In the centre of the hall upon the second landing was running water and a washing place. The average native bath is not taken in a tub all at once, as we do, but less water is used with much soaping, scrubbing and rinsing. The other room on the second floor was a kitchen, where many things to eat were preserved in earthen jars, the whole pervaded by the strong rancid odour of cheese. The water-buffalo milk and the goat milk are too strong for the average American nostril. This class of Egyptian lives well, has an abundance and variety of meat, cheese, vegetables and fruits. There was no dining-room with a table set for a meal, and chairs around it, but the food is brought and eaten when needed.

A small chest stood in one corner and from this the good lady began to exhibit her treasures—an elaborate necklace of gold coins, some other gold coins, two braided gold bracelets, some strings of beads and rings of gold.

Then came the dresses, a dozen or more, evidently dating from her wedding. Then two beautiful gold and silver *galabeyeh* which the hostess tried to throw around me and, with a truly Bedouin gesture, offered it to me. She tried to fasten the bracelets upon my wrists and adjust the necklace. Although we had no common medium of language, we made ourselves understood by signs and smiles. I stood, or sat upon one of the beds, while she, with a baby always draped upon her hip, also stood, or squatted upon the tiles. She wore amber and silver anklets, no stockings, and the long black garments and head wrap of the peasant woman. Her face was tattooed on the chin and forehead.

Sitt Abouka, endeavouring to entertain me to the limit of her powers, produced her make-up box, and showed me how to put on the kohl about the eyes with a long silver needle, as well as the rouge high on the cheeks. She, apparently, was not troubled by any idea of germs, and asked me in the most friendly way to share her things. A truly charming person, and I got a glimpse of the gossipy, cosy times the women of this class must have together. Those I have met all seem very gentle and amiable. She gave me a string of authentic mummy beads, and I in turn gave her a cut-crystal and jade necklace, and also added to her collection of gold pieces, one from the United States Mint.

When Sitt Abouka was asked if she was happy, she replied, "Why not? My husband has but one wife. I have several boys and a nice house and am comfortable, and may Allah give us long life!"

CHAPTER XI

THE home of the lower *bourgeoisie* has progressed considerably towards our standards.

At the French Consulate at Luxor, where I was invited for coffee one afternoon at five, I found two soft-voiced women speaking English, Evelyn Bishara and her cousin, Moneera Elias. Mlle. Bishara had been educated at the American Mission where there are about 200 girls yearly, who receive a liberal education in arithmetic, Arabic, Domestic Science, history, geography, astronomy. A small boy, a brother, took my card and soon re-appeared with it asking me to step upstairs. I noticed the huge trunk of a date palm growing in the hall right up two stories and going through a hole in the roof where its waving graceful fronds afforded both shade and dates for the family! I saw two good-sized public rooms with sofas and chairs arranged against the walls, the first swathed in linen covers, the second Moorish style with turned spindles and plush seats and many embroidered pillows, these last the handwork of Evelyn, the daughter of the house.

Girls marry later now that education develops their individualities and helps them to realize more of life. Evelyn's mother married at 12, while she is 19 and not even engaged, and Moneera is 21 and unmarried, although her mother was a wife at 7! Girls are now con-

[93]

sulted and cannot be married against their will, and they are now allowed to see their fiancés before marriage, which is quite an innovation. When I asked them about their interest in Egypt's Independence, these girls grew very serious and Evelyn said: "The women of Luxor are not organized as well as in Cairo. We cannot do much, but we pray many times a day for our country's freedom. We know the English have done wonderful things for our country, but we want the Europeans as our guests, not our rulers. We pray always for it. There is much power in prayer," she added in conclusion.

The family eat together, European style, wash their hands and pray before each meal and at night, Oriental style. This family follow the Coptic Religion.

They go to church morning and afternoon, the women in a separate part. "But," Evelyn hastened to add, "now there is a church in Cairo, built by the sons of Boutros Ghali Pasha as a memorial to him, where the women are on one side of the church and the men on the other, like Quaker churches."

These girls have more liberty than their mothers, but they do not mingle with men freely as in our country. They do not go to theatres "because they would hear things not good." The women of their class go to the cinemas, but not to restaurants with their husbands, although they know that all this is done in Cairo and Alexandria, which cities lead Egypt, and are waiting for the greater freedom to extend to the Provinces.

These women go to friends' houses with their men-folk. They read and sew and help with the housework, overseeing the servants. We were asked to write in a guest-book.

THE CONSUL'S DAUGHTER

The girls asked about our short skirts and low necks and peek-a-boo waists in America.   I asked if they would go out in a *felucca* alone with a young man, to which they shook their heads.

"Young girls have a better time in your country, but as we become educated all this will change," said Moneera, sagely.

The large square house of yellow stucco has a walled garden and the family sleep on the roof most of the year. A pleasant life this, which knows the waxing and waning of the moon, the upgetting and downgoing of the sun, and even a little of the rise and fall of empires.   The whirr of women's entrance into public life has penetrated even to this calm roof, where date palms wave and earnest young hearts pray for the freedom and glory of their country.

CHAPTER XII

THE AMERICAN MISSION

AS Evelyn and Moneera are examples of what the American Mission is doing in Egypt, it is interesting to note briefly a few outlines of this monument to the power of religion and response to the Christ call, "Go ye unto all the world and preach the Gospel to every creature."

The Madrasset el-Imrican (American School) is established in 175 villages from the college at Assuit with 700 students, and the Pressley Institute with 400 girls, to the pioneer work in mud-brick villages. This enterprise, under the United Presbyterian Churches of America, began nearly seven decades ago. Hundreds of lives and millions of dollars have been invested in it. The care of the body, mind and soul have been carried on together, American medical care is available in two well-appointed American hospitals at Tanta which is the third city of Egypt, between Cairo and Alexandria, and at Assuit which is the centre of Middle Egypt.

The greeting here quoted from a booklet, "America in Egypt," gives an idea of the genial spirit in which this work is conducted:

TO THOSE AMERICANS who take pride in the overseas acomplishments of their fellow-countrymen, and
TO THE TRAVELLERS, of whatever nation, who wish to escape for a time from the ordinary paths, and

THE AMERICAN MISSION

TO ALL WHO wish to see what Americans are doing in Egypt—whether conducting a college with 700 students or acting as evangelists in mud-brick villages:

JUST FOLKS—NO HALOS

The 172 Americans—ministers, doctors, nurses and teachers, and the wives of missionaries—are just folks, like those at home. Some have been here for 60 days and some for 60 years. The missionaries live here seven years at a time, then have a year in America. Their work familiarizes them with Real Egypt, which lies just around the corner, so they become members of city councils, counsellors in important civic and ecclesiastical tours, preside over a college or drink cinnamon tea in the poorest home in a village with equal facility. There isn't a halo in any of the Mission's equipment.

The aim of the mission is to train, educate and Christianize—not Westernize—this most hospitable and interesting people.

In Cairo, the metropolis of Egypt, the American personnel is seventy, housed in the Central Building, opposite Shepheard's.

Two thousand pupils in mission schools and colleges daily; regular preaching in 20 congregations or other groups every Sabbath; a dozen Bible women engaged in *harîm* work—these facts give some idea of the extent of American mission work in Cairo alone, which ranges from street Sabbath schools to the highest-class girl's college and a theological seminary. Here, too, are a half-dozen veteran missionaries whose stories of the early mission days read like romances.

The Pressley Institute is a school of Higher Learning

for Girls, founded in 1865, and has trained thousands of Upper Egypt girls of all classes. Many of them are from the "best families" and a Special Department has been provided for their needs. The yearly enrollment is about 400, nearly half of these are boarders from over 50 towns. The school tries to fit the students to serve Egypt by providing classes in Normal Training and Domestic Science, as well as the usual curriculum, and has long since outgrown its present quarters.

Many Moslems are reached as well as Copts. The non-Mohammedans, naturally, take more rapidly to the religious teaching, which, however, is not forced upon students, and there are no restrictions laid upon students practising their own creeds.

In Northern Egypt, from Cairo to the Sea, there are 31 schools under the care and auspices of the Mission. In them are 2,000 boys and 1,500 girls. Many of them are Moslems, for this territory is much more than nine-tenths Mohammedan.

These schools are scattered all through the Delta. Wherever the missionary or evangelist visits, he finds young men and women friends who receive the workers kindly, and through whom meetings are arranged. Far-reaching is the help given by these most important "lighthouses."

Egypt has been likened to a palm tree, its root at Assuan, its foliage the Delta, and its fruit, as a bunch of dates, the Fayum. Everywhere has the sap of the American Mission penetrated. A brief description of the school which Evelyn and Moneera attended will give an example of the whole.

Embowered in the graceful foliage of the date palm on

THE AMERICAN MISSION

the road to Karnak and its past glories, stands the School for Girls of the American Mission at Luxor. Opposite, on the shady road, so grateful to the sun-tried traveller, two men in the native long-flowing *galabeyeh* were making rope—they did not require a rope walk, an overseer and a timekeeper, but, with the casual manner belonging to the East, were squatted unconcernedly upon some one else's ground and using both feet as well as hands and chest to twist the hempen strands. The *bowab* of the Mission, who combined the offices of gatekeeper and handy man between dawn and dusk, was employing some of the many leisure moments which he took during the day's work, in retailing a choice bit of information that an American lady was being shown over the school and was going to tell her people about it, the people who live in rich houses where everything is done by machinery and nobody has to work. It was an example of the grapevine telegraph in action. Through the morning many natives passing on this busy road which connects Luxor with outlying villages, would stop to pass the word with the rope makers and in turn would be given this titbit.

The Mission is built on three sides of a garden square, is two stories high with balconies and a flat roof.

It was Sunday morning, and about two hundred native girls of all shades of religions and classes were assembled in the spacious cool chapel.

The 127th Psalm was sung in Arabic to an Arabic tune, then an English air, a few Sunday School songs in English, and "My Country 'tis of Thee" in Arabic. It was a strange sight—these dusky girls often very good looking, of an Oriental land, singing American songs in their

[99]

A WOMAN TENDERFOOT IN EGYPT

own language. It was just another contrast in this land of contrasts.

At the Mission the boarders do the waiting on table, bed-making, dish-washing and most of the cooking. These things are part of their training. Much oil is used, instead of butter, and the native bean, *fuhl medernis,* is a staple article of diet. Kerosene is now beginning to be used for fuel, for wood is precious. $60 provides board and tuition, and another $15 is supposed to furnish the clothing. The daughter of a pasha or a bey (upper class titles corresponding roughly to Lord and Sir), and the second class boarders pay $80 per term. Music is available for $20 a term extra. The native teacher's salary is $25 per month. The school is provided with modern plumbing arrangements. The proper use of these and of the weekly bath is taught at the same time as the three R's. The peasants do not understand plumbing and think it silly. Some of the upper class girls have even to learn the correct use of knife, fork and spoon. The lower class habit is to dip the fingers into a common food pot. The dormitories are clean and airy. Each girl has an iron bed, canopied with netting for flies and gnats. In place of springs the mattress is placed on boards, as the majority of girls are accustomed to the unyielding ground to sleep upon, and are not comfortable on springs!

The superintendent, Miss Ida Whiteside, who is also a nurse, related an incident when she was in the hospital at Assuit. A peasant woman, very ill in a high fever, was brought in and put to bed. Shortly after, in making the rounds, the nurse was alarmed to see an empty bed where she had lately placed the new-comer. She soon discovered her very sick patient lying without covers on the tile floor under the bed. The poor woman had to have her mattress put on boards as she complained that she could not rest on a thing that jumped up and down.

The Girls' School begins in August and closes in May, which allows the American personnel some relief from the extreme heat of summer, when they get three months' vacation. The salary is the princely sum of $500 a year and board, truly a labor of love for the land. Many native teachers are graduated each year, which provides an ever increasing number of the Spreaders of Light.

CHAPTER XIII

THE STORY OF SITT ESSA

IT was at this American Mission School for Girls at Luxor that I first made the acquaintance of the slave girl, Sitt Essa, standing in the door of her kitchen. She represents the last frontier to be reached by the onward march of education. Her name was Essa and the courtesy title of Sitt was added by these kindly women, as their cook had come from a family of good degree in her Sudanese village. Her rotund form was clad in American calico, a native black shawl draped her head and outlined a face round, happy and black, with three scar gashes on the right cheek. Those gashes told the story of capture, terror, torture, now 35 years old, of a night when she was torn from her native village in the Sudan, put upon a slave boat and mutilated for all her life. Her rescue was a romance.

A third of a century ago on a certain moonless night, one of the three missionary boats which the American Mission in Egypt has kept plying on the Nile for sixty years, tied up for the night by the side of another boat near Luxor on the bank of this strange river, where boats at times have to be towed down stream, and into whose muddy waters living creatures, from animals to beautiful young virgins, were, in bygone days, sacrificed to the Nile God.

The strange boat proved to be a slaver from the Su-

dan. Five of the miserable young girls upon it succeeded in escaping and creeping along in the darkness,
when even the stars grew dim, they reached the American
dahabeyeh and appealed to the Missionary for protection. He promptly took them to the Girls' Mission at
Luxor where Miss McGowan, in charge, gave them refuge,
fed and clothed them. When the villainous slave dealer
early next morning, whip in hand, sought his property,
she defied him courageously. The English had already
made slave-dealing a crime, so this little woman, for the
moment without help other than her five dusky charges
cowering behind her, pluckily bade the irate trafficker of
human bodies and souls to depart, or take the conse-
quences of the law. He retired in bad order, and left
hastily with his *dahabeyeh* for Assuit, while Miss Mc-
Gowan was urging the native authorities to act in the
matter.

The other girls were eventually returned to their
homes, but Sitt Essa, by the time that was possible, had
become so attached to her Mission home that she preferred to stay where she could "cook the food and bless
the Lord" at the same time. Looking at her disfigured
cheek and remembering that slavery in our own country
was hardly extinct 55 years ago, I left her neat kitchen,
her smiling face and gentle eyes, with a deep wonder that
humanity finds it so hard to learn the lesson of love and
co-operation—which makes to blossom the waste places
of the soul.

CHAPTER XIV

FRENCH MISSIONS, EGYPTIAN SCHOOLS AND OTHER EDUCATIONAL FRONTIERS

THE French Missions are also a very powerful educational factor in Egypt, and now there are some purely Egyptian institutions—such as the Girls' Academy in Minia in Upper Egypt, which is conducted by Madame Fekrich Horny. The curriculum is arranged for undergraduate work for girls coming from elementary schools of Upper Egypt. It includes arithmetic, Arabic, English, French, geography, hygiene, domestic science, history, nature study. Under this heading, I received a thrill when the dark-eyed, gentle-voiced little woman told me she had travelled far to meet the wife of the author whose books she was using for Nature Study and English. There is also a course in Kindergarten work to train teachers for the elementary schools. This is the direct result of the New Woman influence.

The school has accommodation for 51 girls; more are taken under 13 years of age, and the demand is greatly in excess of that number. This college would grow, but is hampered for funds and the buildings are inadequate. There is a staff of four women teachers, two Sheikhs, a clerk and the Head-mistress. Madame Horny seemed surprised when I asked if the parents offered any objection to their daughters being taught by the Sheikhs.

EDUCATIONAL FRONTIERS

"Ah, no, they are very fine men. The girls are not *purdah* (secluded)."

The girls of the upper stratum of the pasha class are still privately educated and very well educated by governesses, and allowed to go to convents and European schools and colleges. The public school system of Kenia Province was described to me by the Sub-Mudir, M. Fathy Bey who lives below Luxor.

The educational system in the Kenia Province, which has six districts of which Luxor is one, provides for two primary schools to each district, one for girls and one for boys; about eight boys out of 1,000 go to school, and not even that proportion of girls. The peasants take no interest in the education of the children. But all are taxed five per cent. of the income on a feddan of land for schooling that goes into a fund administered by a council which directs these schools. Then there are the elementary schools, one each for girls and boys in each district, and the parents must pay, besides their taxes, about $25 a year tuition fee for each child, though there are some free classes. In addition there are the sectarian schools for Copts, Protestants and Catholics, French and Italian, maintained by the followers of these religions where any one may go, who can qualify. They are for the better class, of both sexes, who are educated separately. Finally there are some colleges, privately endowed.

All this effort towards education, and more, is needed, for there is no doubt that Egypt, like Italy, suffers from the reproach of illiteracy. The latest statistics give only six or seven per cent. of the Egyptian population of nearly 14 millions as being able to read and write. In

A WOMAN TENDERFOOT IN EGYPT

Cairo, with its large Western population, half the male population is totally uneducated, and only 42,000 women and girls, excluding those aged less than five, of the 277,000 in the city are literate.

There are villages of 5,000 inhabitants in which not a woman can read and write—so the census states—with perhaps a score of men able to do so. However, these conditions have been very much bettered in the ten years which have elapsed since the last census.

A native lawyer who has been studying the subject lately puts the figure of illiteracy at ninety per cent. He claims that while the population during the past forty years under English occupancy and Protectorate has practically doubled, the percentage of literacy has not increased, indeed has decreased since the time of Ismail, when education was compulsory for at least a portion of the community. Egypt itself is becoming awake to the necessity of education for girls as well as boys, and there is no longer much difficulty in persuading parents to send their children to school, especially among the Copts, who avail themselves of the excellent French and American Missions located all along the Nile. And there are also governmental schools in all the Provinces.

Among the Moslems of the lower classes, the matter is not so easy. The priests discourage female education, but they are gradually having to yield to public opinion.

Abdur Rahman Ismail published in 1909 in Cairo a naïve primer on Moslem Ethics for use in the schools in which he attempts to readjust them to Christian standards.

And Ata Husain Bey of Cairo recently published an

EDUCATIONAL FRONTIERS

account of a Moslem Educational Conference held at Delhi in 1911, when Her Highness the Begum of Bhopal made a strong appeal for the education of Moslem Girls, in the following terms: "Girls of today will be mothers of the future and have to bear the whole community. The neglect of the men for the women's condition and their continued ignorance works even more disadvantageously for the men than for the women. A leader of the Persian Parliament said recently to Dr. Esselstyn: 'The hope of our country is in the education of the girls, and we can never have statesmen till the mothers are educated.' "

Among the middle and upper classes, where the parents can afford it, the girls are given an excellent education at home in languages, sciences, religion and politics. At least, if politics are not taught they are acquired, for I have been astonished at the political interest and information of the present generation, not only about their own country and its struggle for Independence, but about contemporary political history elsewhere. Perhaps the psychology of it is the same as I have observed at isolated army posts in America where the degree of up-to-date knowledge of the world's current output of music, literature and the arts has often surprised and charmed me. Once when my hostess, the wife of an Army officer stationed at an out-of-the-way post in the Rockies, asked me about a certain play, then running simultaneously in New York and London and I had to confess that I had not even heard of it, she remarked, "Oh, well, you see, here we feel so out of it that we make a special effort to keep up."

The weekly illustrated journal, *The Woman's World,*

published in Constantinople for Moslem womanhood, has a large circulation in Egypt. And recent books like "The Women and the Work," written by an Egyptian woman, Nabuwey a Mousa, are fulfilling their mission of spreading modern ideas through the printed word.

The itch for knowledge and a larger expression, both national and individual, has certainly urged Egypt onto the world's stage and, in the growing freedom, her women have no intention of being left behind—let her be the daughter of the wealthy Moslem in Cairo, or of the middle-class Copt in the Provinces, or the bride of a Bedouin Sheikh, who promised me solemnly that her first-born, boy or girl, should be sent to school. The torch of knowledge, which unites all peoples, has been lighted in the land of the Pharaohs.

BOOK I

PART III

A SOLDIER-STATESMAN

Field-Marshal Viscount Allenby, G. C. B., G. C. M. G.,
etc.

CHAPTER XV

ON the Nile today is being played a fascinating game of National chess. The Red pawns are the Egyptian people. The White Pieces have taken most of the Red Pieces. But sometimes the God of Things-As-They-Are helps the Red side to make a Sicilian Defence which puts the White "King" in check. The Capablanca of the Game is Field-Marshal Viscount Allenby of Megiddo and Felixstowe, G.C.B., G.C.M.G., etc., British High-Commissioner for Egypt and the Sudan.

In the preceding chapters these moves have been touched upon sufficiently to give a background to this famous Soldier-Statesman when, in the early spring of 1922, His Excellency received me at the Residency in Cairo.

But one most important factor, the "Castle," among the White Pieces, must be described, before I can present the particular section of the Game, which I was able to observe at first-hand, when the Wizard invited my presence in his study, on the day of his departure for England to present the Egyptian problem and his suggested solution to "Downing Street."

This important "piece" is the Commander-in-Chief of the British Expeditionary Force in Egypt—Lieutenant-

A WOMAN TENDERFOOT IN EGYPT

General Sir Walter Congreve, V.C., K.C.B., and a long string of other titles. His part in Anglo-Egyptian affairs is second only to that of Lord Allenby, who acts as an administrator, while General Congreve is in charge of all military operations. I first saw him as a genial host, of some 60 summers, in a large house, surrounded by gardens, on the Island of Gezireh, next to the English Country Club. As a junior officer he won the Victoria Cross at the Battle of Colenso in the South African War, an example to be followed 16 years later by his son, the late Major William La Touche Congreve, of the Rifle Brigade, who won the same coveted distinction at the Battle of Saint-Eloi, near Ypres, on March 30th, 1916, an unusual honour for both father and son! The only other example in history was Lord Roberts and his heir.

General Congreve's son, "Billy," as he was affectionately known among his brother officers, was one of the most brilliant young soldiers in the British Army. Before he was twenty-five, he was the possessor of the V. C. (awarded however, posthumously), the D. S. O., the M. C. and the Legion of Honour, and was slated for the command of a brigade when his career was cut short by a German sniper at the Somme, about the 10th of July, 1916, just one month after his marriage to Pamela Maude, daughter of the famous English actor, Cyril Maude. A son to be proud of, and to mourn.

This was not the only sacrifice Sir Walter Congreve has made for the country he serves so well—his right sleeve hangs empty. Of thin and wiry build, with a soldier's directness, he belongs to the fearless, executive type which has made the British Army what it is today.

Lady Congreve, daughter of Captain C. B. La Touche,

and author of a recently-published, "Garland of Verse," of delightful quality and freshness, is a tall, graceful, Englishwoman, who bears her share of the social duties and pleasures of her husband's position and brings an observant mind to bear upon the conditions of Egypt from her standpoint. Some of her comments on the night I dined with the Commander-in-Chief and his Lady, are given, as representative of the opinion of the cultured British Colony.

Lady Congreve said: "Many of the Copts ape the Mohammedans and lead the *purdah* life. The Princess Fewkie, daughter of King Fuad I, lives many months in Paris each year, a normal existence, has many friends among men, but when she returns to Alexandria or Cairo, she retires from them all and lives *'la vie grotesque,'* as she calls it, of seclusion and the veil. I know a number of the Royal princesses; they, come to my house on special occasions, and even to dine. I am careful what men I have, but these women are not so strict about the veiling as they used to be. They are all charming, and all speak French.

"In the Queen's Palace of Abdin lives the Queen, a great lady, but isolated, meeting no man but her husband, who has but her for wife. She has two young children, the last one a baby from whose birth she has not yet fully recovered, and two ladies-in-waiting and a number of servants, but no large entourage. She gives audience occasionally to wives of officials and of officers and, very rarely, to visiting women foreigners.

"Occasionally now the Mohammedan lady is seen in public with her husband. This is a great innovation: and from time to time a very bold group of women forms a modern delegation to a man in authority, in the effort for greater freedom.

"Until the Egyptian has learned to give to his women a normal, modern life, how can he hope to govern himself successfully?

"What is to be expected in a country which maltreats its animals and permits such methods of living?

"All the hygienic conditions of this very modern city are due to the English, the roads, the street lights, modern bridges, buildings, policing. I cannot think what would happen to them if we let go."

General Congreve's comment to this, was:

"Even the educated Turk and Egyptian is no match for the Arabs who would swarm in upon them if the English were removed. Oxford- or Cambridge-bred Egyptians are no rarity, but, even so, they have not the *flair* for Government at present.   •

"There is no danger for foreigners in Cairo," he added, in response to my question—for the "tourist" is filled with strange stories—"if people stick to the main thoroughfares. Even in New York and London there are sections where one would not be safe."

When asked about the riots and the Zaghlulists, the General said: "Mme. Zaghlul is very quiet just now." (Meaning that she was not causing trouble at that time.)

Lady Congreve's idea of it was, "Madame Zaghlul Pasha is working purely for political reasons. If what you say is true, and I thought she was interesting herself for the advancement of women, I should be very glad indeed."

The Military Governor of Palestine, of the usual tall, well-built British-officer type, and Mrs. Wardrop, were visiting the Congreves for a week, while an Officers' School was being conducted at Cairo Barracks, for the purpose of brushing up-to-date the officers of the Northern African Section. There is no slackness allowed to creep into the British Army under General Congreve, who is an executive soldier, first and always. Indeed no officer in the British Expeditionary Forces is more highly respected.

"We all have to go to school as long as we live; or else we are dead, no matter how long we live," was his whimsical pronouncement. General Wardrop nodded approvingly.

"Perhaps you will be coming to Palestine?" he questioned. "There is now an aërial post, eleven hours flying time from Cairo to Bagdad and eighteen hours lands you in Jerusalem."

"Wonderful—a ship in the air instead of a ship of the Desert. Are you going home that way?"

"No, I think we shall try to keep our feet on the ground."

The meaning of this was clear. The Commanding Officer of Palestine has not a bed of roses, either; but, as Kipling says, "that is another story."

General Congreve's particular thorns are rebellion, disorder and bloodshed.

It chanced that I was in the drawing-room of an Anglo-Egyptian Official, the Head Surgeon of the Kasr-el-Aine Hospital, on the preceding day, when a particularly disconcerting murder of an English Railway Official had been committed by a native within pistol shot of the apartment house where I was taking tea. Policemen were patrolling the streets in front of this house as I went in.

A WOMAN TENDERFOOT IN EGYPT

It was grotesquely like locking the stable door after the horse was stolen, for the assailant had done his deed, hours before, at a purely accidental spot, and the police were merely "rolling their tub" in guarding the locality.

A prominent Englishman summed up Lord Allenby's policy at this time. It was: first, to abolish Military Law; second, to withdraw the Protectorate; third, to establish two Houses of Parliament and a Cabinet responsible to them with the Sultan, as King. Perhaps even to allow ambassadors abroad: and let the Egyptians have a try at governing themselves. If they can, well and good: they will be given a chance. But on the other hand, not to withdraw all at once, but await results. To return, a High Commissioner, for a time with a sufficient number of troops to enable him to protect British interests in Egypt, the Suez Canal and the Sudan; as well as the European and other interests, which should be safeguarded.

I was on wire edge to meet the man who held Egypt in the hollow of his hand, and about whom, not even from an Egyptian, had I heard a derogatory word.

The appointment had been made for February 1, 1922, through the American Diplomatic Agent, Dr. J. Morton Howell, who sent word that His Excellency would see me at eleven, and that if I would appear at the Consulate at 10.45 he would accompany me. I was a few minutes early, and waited in the garden, among the roses and oleanders, where several Arabs were working, until a musical, masculine voice behind me announced the advent of Uncle Sam's representative. I turned to see a gentleman who bore a striking resemblance to President Harding. Indeed he is another son of Ohio, having been born in Dayton about sixty years ago. A thick crop of snow-white hair, a ruddy, massive face and kindly, keen eyes, a tall, well-built figure in a grey suit. A generous button-hole of fresh violets and a suggestion of lavender handkerchief completed the picture.

The American Legation in Cairo is a large, rambling structure on two sides of an open garden which is charming with flowers and grass plots laid out formally. Dr. J. Morton Howell, only a few weeks in his post, had worked wonders in the house and grounds which had been allowed to run down. The large ballroom and state dining-room and drawing-room had been redecorated and made available for the first official function of the Howells, which took place on Washington's Birthday, when the English and American colonies and the Egyptian Officials attended. A diplomat's wife is important in any country, but nowhere more necessary than in a Moslem country where sex is still a social problem, and Mrs. Howell does her share.

Dr. Howell's first impressions included the following (I wonder what he thinks now after a year or two in this hot-bed of the changing East): "Egypt is becoming more and more important to America, commercially, and Egypt needs American enterprise. The Egyptians are not yet ready to govern themselves. They cannot well form a Ministry alone. They have been very sick—they are still very sick. What is the matter after 40 years of British influence? Let us look at the laboratory and see the cause of this weakness."

"Perhaps it is the Turk germs," I ventured.

"Yes, another name for it, perhaps. The matter is *IGNORANCE*. Establish schools and go among the villages and make the father and mother realize that they must send their children to school *every day*. The parents are hopeless, but that is the only way out for Egypt. *Education* in the Elementary branches and in Hygiene. But they are a most fascinating people. I like them."

The American Diplomatic Agent in Eygpt at this time had the standing and privilege of a minister. "So long as there is a British Protectorate it is not much use raising the Agency to a Legation," was his comment. This was done, however, soon after, in June, 1922, and Dr. Howell was appointed by President Harding, American Minister to the newly-created Court of King Fuad I. of Egypt.

As we walked across to the opposite corner where the palatial buildings of the Residency are set in extensive grounds, terraced down to the Nile, we discussed the Field-Marshal's war record. As Commander of the Cavalry Corps he fought throughout the First Battle of Ypres (1914), then held the Command, first of the Fifth Army Corps, then of the Third Army, which he relinquished early in 1917 to General Byng, whereupon he proceeded to Palestine, achieved a great victory over the Turks, and restored the Holy Sepulchre to the Christians, after entering Jerusalem on Dec. 11th, 1917. After the Armistice, he was appointed Special High-Commissioner for Egypt and the Sudan.

Having passed through the imposing flower-bordered entrance of the Residency, Captain B——, Lord Allenby's A. D. C., greeted us at the top of a wide stairway. I just had time to look through the glass, which separated the hall from the brick and marble terrace, beyond to a noble sweep of lawn and tropical trees to the ever-chang-

ing river, now flowing sweetly past as though it never had
vagaries of channels and mudbanks. A dignified palace,
in a beautiful setting, is the Residency.

Almost immediately, as it was on the dot of eleven, the
Aide announced that His Excellency was waiting to see
me.

We were ushered into a spacious, well-furnished room.
In the center was a large desk from which Lord Allenby
arose, extending a cordial hand.

Seldom does one have the satisfaction, shall I say the
thrill, of meeting a person whose achievements have compelled our admiration and who measures up to the heroic picture that has been built up in one's imagination.

Viscount Allenby looks, acts, and is, the part of the
hero of Palestine, and of the brilliant statesman-soldier
of troubled Egypt. He was dressed in dark blue "civ-
vies," and, I think, a blue four-in-hand sprinkled with
tiny polka-dots. I am not sure of this, for I was so
busy looking at his face, which fascinated by its contrasts. The lines of the chin and brow are square, the
nose and mouth firm and well-shaped. The hand of the
potter did not shake when any part of this face, head,
or figure, was moulded. But it was the eyes that held
me. I do not even know their colour—perhaps grey-
blue. It was what looked out of them that occupied my
thoughts—piercing, with steely glints in them, and yet
sunshine flashes of humour, and that rare quality—understanding. The iron will of one accustomed to command looked out of these "windows," the unbending,
unflinching, demand for truth and justice. Also, there
flashed, at times, the spirit of a man unafraid, ready to

[119]

use his sword or his pen in performance of his duty, but who knows his fellow-man to be a mixture of God and the Devil, and that no man can read the Book of Fate.

He expressed himself very glad to meet me on my own account and on account of my husband, about whose works he made some very flattering remarks. "The Chief," he added, did a great thing for the youth of America when he started the outdoor movement. Baden-Powell owes much to him. We have a lively group of Boy Scouts here."

Then it was my turn:

"I have asked to meet your Excellency as you are the most commanding figure in Egypt, and of what value would be impressions of Egypt with Lord Allenby left out? Also because I have a very great admiration of your prowess and skill as a soldier and statesman, and now that I have met you I am not disappointed in my mental pictures of you."

At this point the great man actually blushed.

"If you go on like this I shall not be able to stand it," he protested.

I told him that H. G. Wells had said of Mrs. Pankhurst that the Government had given English women the vote because "We could not have two wars on our hands." Lord Allenby laughed. "Wells is a great boy. No, I am not a suffragist, nor am I against woman's suffrage! I am neutral."

I then asked him if he could tell me about the women in Egypt. He said, "I do not think they have come out of the *purdah* condition, nor do they want to, except perhaps a few who are interested in politics." Alas, I was discovering the Achilles heel of my hero. Did he know anything of "La Femme Nouvelle"? I asked him, and he looked vague.

"But Madame Zaghlul Pasha!" I exclaimed. "Surely she is doing wonders towards the greater freedom of women?"

There was an instant's pause. "Zaghlul?" questioned Lord Allenby, *"Who is she?"*

The face wore an expression of gracious interest. One could write volumes and not better express the power of the man, his astuteness and fitness for the difficult post where the hand of Providence has placed him. I almost caught my breath with surprise, but was quick enough on the uptake to answer in the same vein:

"Why, Madame Zaghlul is a lady who has helped her husband with the Nationalist movement here. It is a matter of no importance, of course."

"No—a matter of no importance," said the High Commissioner of Egypt, sweetly.

Madame Zaghlul Pasha, "who is she?" indeed! The woman who had defied him—him, the all-powerful. The woman who had said to him over the 'phone, "You may banish, you may kill Saad Pasha—but Saad lives here in Egypt so long as *I*, his wife, can live!" The British Soldier-Conqueror is not fighting women. "Zaghlul, who is she?" He has adopted a much cleverer policy—that of attenuation. He ignores, so far as possible, a situation with which he does not care to deal. But the "disturbances" still go on, for the Egyptian people do not mourn their banished leader quietly.

Some details of commercial importance to America and Egypt were discussed with Dr. Howell before me for a few moments, as, in a dozen hours, the High Commissioner would be on the Mediterranean and absent from his post for three weeks; perhaps, if the Foreign Office did not see his point—for ever. A hundred matters pressed for his attention, but there was no hint of this, other than his Aide's slipping into the room several times, laying a message on the desk, and going quietly out again.

"I hope," said Lord Allenby, "that you will be here some time. It may be I can show you some matters that will interest you—when I return—if all goes well."

Rising to his vigorous, broad-shouldered, military height, Lord Allenby bent a clear, twinkling blue eye upon me:

"If you are interested in women, you should find some excellent material here. Thank you for coming, and may we meet again soon."

A handshake and a bow and we gave place to the next caller, who was none other than the remarkable publisher of the London *Times,* and a host of other papers, an interesting world-figure, who so soon afterwards, alas! was to close his career—too quickly burnt out at fifty-seven. During the Great War I was the recipient of many kindly acts by this man whose death made a dent in the civilized world consciousness. Next to Lloyd George, he was, perhaps, the most important Englishman as a shaper of policies during the Great War. On that day Lord Northcliffe was the "busiest man in Cairo." He was endeavouring to get a bird's-eye view of the Egyptian situation in three days at the fag-end of his famous hustle around the world.

When I returned to the hotel I found the following letter which, had it arrived earlier, I could not have reproduced here, and never was able to deliver, as the steamer which brought Lord Allenby back to Egypt, his mission successfully accomplished, took me, a reluctant passenger, out of the country.

GENERAL OF THE ARMIES
WASHINGTON

January 31, 1922.

Field Marshal Sir Edmund H. Allenby,
    The Residency,
        Cairo, Egypt.

My dear Field Marshal:

      I am taking the liberty of commending to your good offices one of our foremost American writers, Mrs. Ernest Thompson Seton, who is going to Cairo to do some research work. Mrs. Seton was connected with the British Ministry of Information, American Section, during the war and any courtesies you may be able to extend to her will be greatly appreciated by me.

      Believe me, my dear Field Marshal, with high esteem and cordial personal regards,

      Yours very sincerely,

John J. Pershing

[123]

A WOMAN TENDERFOOT IN EGYPT

Under Egypt's new régime, Lord Allenby's title of High Commissioner is changed to *Mandub-es-Sami,* which literally means "very high delegate." As the conqueror of the Sudan, Lord Kitchener, laboured over the Egyptian Volcano to keep quiet the seething mass of irreconcilables, so the Conqueror of Palestine, whom the Arabs considered as a sort of Messiah from the anagram on his name, Ibn-ben-Allah—son of Allah, now "sits on the lid," a sagacious, kindly arbiter. Egypt's future is on the knees of the Gods.

BOOK I

PART IV

ANGLO-EGYPTIAN ANGLES

CHAPTER XVI

ANGLO-EGYPTIAN ANGLES

WHATEVER one may think of the attitude of the British in Egypt, it springs from a settled policy of colonization. They honestly believe that they could not with safety "mix with the natives," on terms of social equality, nor can they entirely "get out of Egypt," thus throwing her into the International Hornets' Nest only to have the prize carried off by some other Power.

Robert V. Dolbey, M.C., M.V.O., F.R.C.S., Head Surgeon of the biggest hospital in Cairo, the Kasr-el-Aine, discussed the subject in the fair-minded attitude one is accustomed to associate with the British character. "I do not blame the high-class Egyptian for resenting us, and our attitude of exclusion and superiority. We must seem arrogant, for we will not open our houses and our clubs to them. The Oriental traits make this unwise. The Oriental man is keen about the white woman. If he marries her, as he occasionally does, his standards are such that he soon degrades her; and of course we are not going to let our women—our wives and sisters and sweethearts— have anything to do with them.

"I believe that the Egyptian is not capable of carrying on a modern government. But one cannot but sympathize with the educated Egyptian who sees himself set aside for the foreigner. During the Great War the Egyp-

[127]

tians gave us wheat and straw in huge quantities and a lot of able-bodied men. Lord Allenby said they were a great help in the winning of Palestine."

Then he said an illuminating thing from the Anglo-Egyptian angle:

"The trouble is that we English in Egypt are trying to graft our 20th century civilization upon 14th century conditions. Of course some of the upper and middle class Egyptians are Europeanized, especially in Cairo and Alexandria; they have and use bathrooms, the men and women of the family eat together, using table furniture, etc., and if you go into their homes by invitation that is what you will find, a European tea and table service. But, catch them unawares," he continued "in the Provinces, the barriers down by sickness, and you will find the Bey or Pasha in a *galabeyeh*. At meals the men, even down to the boy of 10, sit down at a table after first washing their hands, and tear at their food with their fingers. Without knives or forks they tear apart a turkey, for example, and when they have had their fill, they leave, and the women of the household come and take the leavings. They, too, help themselves to the scraps with their fingers, and after them, the servants come and finish off what is left. These women rarely wear stockings, or take a bath, and sanitary arrangements as we know them are lacking. But there is no doubt a great change taking place."

Egypt, like the rest of the world, is yet in the making. Some women tear at their food with their fingers in Egypt. Other women from America, as we have noted elsewhere, force themselves into a foreign home and are equally lacking in the manners of good society.

ANGLO-EGYPTIAN ANGLES

My own experience, which covered every type of home in Egypt, convinces me that the extent of "Europeanization" is much wider than the good doctor knows of, being a man, and, even as a doctor, rarely admitted to the home; and that it has spread out of the cities into the Provinces, as well.

Mr. Dolbey, who is the author of a war book of personal experiences, "A Regimental Surgeon in War and Prison," and who also saw several years of service in India, has made a study of two miseries of Oriental womankind—the drug habit and "The White Man's Curse—" and has come to the deduction that the two go together and are the result of the abnormal conditions imposed upon the women of Moslem countries. The enforced idleness and seclusion, and the consequent boredom, result in abnormal practices; and the drug habit and the easy divorce often throw on the streets, a woman whose previous training has fitted her to earn her living in only one way. This fills the hospitals with victims.

The main section of the Kasr-el-Aine was built originally by the Khedive Ismail to house his harem of several hundred women—that is, two or three wives, more concubines, and their attendant suites—but was suddenly abandoned at that ruler's downfall in 1870. The hospital, which I visited one morning, has the equipment and organization of a modern British scientific establishment adapted to a warm climate. There are large, cool, cement and tile wards, protected from the weather, on one side, only, by large arches of masonry and striped awnings. The beds are of iron and a little table stands beside each. The convalescent patients squat in groups on rugs of matting on the floor. The sexes are separated.

[129]

A WOMAN TENDERFOOT IN EGYPT

A group of twenty women in one ward were on some rush mats in one corner, chattering quite happily. Some were playing games, others nursing children. None attempted to veil for "the Doctor," although I was told that they were all Moslems.

The English-trained Egyptian makes a good doctor and the Kasr-el-Aine Medical School has many students every year—even a few women have taken the course as noted elsewhere.

There are also English women doctors along the Nile and need for many more. Dr. Maer, who has been doing dispensary work for six years near Assuit, was pessimistic. She and her companion, who has been in Egypt for sixteen years, are too close to the subject to judge of futures. They feel that the native would like to slip back, and that it takes all the effort imaginable to get the money to carry on the dispensary. I have heard the same complaint in similar welfare work in America, England, France and Italy. The workers sometimes cannot see the wood for the trees.

An oasis in the desert of a traveller's job, that of sightseeing, is the glimpse I got of Anglo-Egyptian family life at the home of Mr. H. E. Winlock at Del-el-Beheri—across the River from Luxor. After a grilling day with the Tomb of the Kings, and tombs Nos. 6, 3, 5, 11 and 16 had been duly inspected and thrilled over—and there is no class of impressions comparable to those produced by these marvellous depositories of the dead body and the living soul—the Poet, my delightful companion of travel, and I, climbed a very steep mountain in the broiling sun at high noon and slid and stumbled down the other side in clouds of dust, and heat incredible. Two broiled, purple-faced females arrived at the Cook's Rest House at Del-el-Beheri, and Shehata, the dragoman, lamented that we had refused to order luncheon beforehand. A Cook's party had gobbled up all the food and, more important, all the drink, available. Not a drop of table water was for sale. As usual, Shehata solved the difficulty. I noticed him conversing with a very smart dragoman, who immediately approached a party of three gentlemen, an upper-class Egyptian and two Englishmen. A few words in Arabic and the dragoman began collecting food from the amply-spread board of his master. Then he approached us, with the usual bow.

"His Excellency, the Governor of Kenia, begs that you will partake of this humble food." We accepted the courtesy with much appreciation of the cold chicken and tomatoes and oranges and ginger-ale and with several formal bows to the Sub-Mudir of Kenia.

I was learning the ways of the country and did not at that time venture to shock his Moslem by beginning speech with him.

The Poet bought a bit of old pottery from the clamorous group of vendors of "antiketes," as Shehata called them. It was a piece about five inches high of a female figure, and the colour was a most exquisite green-blue. There was much discussion as to its genuineness, and Shehata took upon himself to consult about this with the handsome Abdul, who proceeded to consult his master the Sub-Mudir, who rendered a verdict in favor of its antiquity. This message was solemnly conveyed to us, although the gentleman made his very audible remarks not eight feet away. Again we acknowledged the courtesy by exchanging bows with the Gentleman from

[131]

A WOMAN TENDERFOOT IN EGYPT

Kenia. The Poet finally bought the piece and paid a good price for it, not because of its recommendations, of which she had doubts, but because the pestiferously-insistent vendor had called it the "Blue Queen." What Poet, with Egyptian pounds in her purse, could withstand owning the "Blue Queen"? Later the Poet proved the antiquity of Her Majesty by dropping her on the bath-room floor where she broke in two on the tiles. The glazes can be imitated, but the peculiar texture of the pottery cannot. Poor Queen! After withstanding the ravages of forty centuries she met her fate on the hard fact of a modern luxury!

Meanwhile the wireless telephone had been working, via the guides, and an invitation arrived to visit Mr. Winlock who had been excavating in this region for six-teen years, and comes under the term "Anglo" only in its broad sense, as he is an American by birth. We lost no time in donkeying to his home, which he has built in the desert. It is an adaptation of the native style of archi-tecture, that combines dome-shaped roofs and arched gal-leries with the needs of an Occidental family. Oriental furniture and draperies, so far as possible, have been used. The house is full of charm. Coffee was served.

Naturally, the discussion turned on the political situa-tion. Everybody talks politics—young and old—the pros and the cons. Everybody knows all about it. Only a few people think they know less. To those, one could sometimes listen with profit and always with interest. Dr. Quibel, a Scotsman, is one of these. He has lived long in Egypt, as Curator of the famous Cairo Museum where one finds untold treasures of the ancient Egyptian glories, owing to the fact that fifty per cent. of all excavated articles must go to the Cairo Museum. Thus the heavy expenses of an expedition are borne by outside enterprise and the Museum grows rapidly in rich acquisitions. He contributes the following ideas.

Since 1885, under the British Occupation, the population has increased thirty per cent. and is now nearly 15 millions, condensed along the Nile, which means about 1,000 persons to the acre. Undoubtedly, the improved conditions brought about by the European influence, not alone British, but also Italian, French and Greek, have reduced the birth rate and enabled the *fellaheen* to grow and enrich. Under Turkish despotism, the upper class, one twenty-fifth of the whole, ruled all the others, and no wonder that this class which is the articulate one, is making a howl for independence, so that they can continue to have the upper hand.

Mr. Winlock had been showing some fascinating results of the recent excavation at the Tomb of Princess Hekht at Del-el-Beheri. It was under his direction that the Metropolitan Museum of New York recently received several invaluable collections of models of boats and industries which reveal whole pages of Egyptian History. These extraordinary discoveries include miniature models of great accuracy and detail which depict the activities of a bygone age, priceless data for the antiquarian and the historian.

He took up the theme:

"One must remember that the Egyptian has been a dominated race for thousands of years while whole nations have risen and triumphed and fallen, and an intellectual facility to twist facts has become an integral part

[133]

of the Egyptian character which cannot be eradicated in a few generations.

"A member of the investigating committee for Lord Milner's Enquiry asked me if I would take an educated, high-class Egyptian on the Excavating work. I replied, 'Certainly not.' To his surprised 'Why not?' I pointed out the trait which would make his co-operation value-less. By intellectual obliqueness I do not mean at all about money matters or stealing—the high-class Egyptians of course would not do that, and many of them are delightful, cultivated people; but that *facility* of mind, which enables an Egyptian, or any Oriental for that matter, however cultivated, to see the thing as he *wants* to see it. For instance with such a man with me, when some relic was discovered, supposing that I was in need of more evidence to prove something, say, that Rameses III. ruled before Rameses II., he would do everything he could to prove it—in order to please me.

"Or, in terms of politics: When Zaghlul Pasha went to London last summer and was there four months and his mission was not progressing, his right-hand man, Adly Pasha, said he was very sorry, but he must return for crops and business, and went home and began getting a following of his own, and he made some dicker with the English about being made Prime Minister, which brought Zaghlul home in a hurry; then Adly Pasha went to Lord Allenby and said he was sorry, but he was afraid to proceed. Then later, he went to London on his own, but his mission was a failure and then Zarwat Pasha slid from the Nationalist party maze and got himself made Prime Minister and he is still in.

"Meanwhile all of the principal members of the Wafd

[134]

who signed the British Boycott manifesto were deported, partly because Zarwat Pasha said he could do nothing about forming a ministry till Zaghlul Pasha was out of the way. Now, do you see what I mean by intellectual gymnastics?"

Dr. Quibel shook his head at this: "That is going a bit too strong. I do not blame the Egyptians for wanting to govern themselves." Then followed the usual arguments.

A charming character is this Dr. Quibel. The harsh qualities of the Scot have been softened by years of life in the East and the sterling qualities which mark a Scotsman are here in abundance. He knows his Egypt, and he loves her, but he is not blind to her faults. He, and his helpmates, are travelling gracefully towards the sunset of life. He observed that the cotton brings the greatest wealth to Egypt, then sugar cane and alfalfa.

The cotton manufacture is not under the Egyptians, although an attempt was made by them to develop this industry, but taxation on the manufactured articles and the competition of the big English mills strangled it at birth. The raw cotton is shipped to Manchester and is returned, British-made, for the Egyptians to buy at a much higher figure; although the cotton trade is largely in the hands of the Greeks.

I had already noticed the Levantines who are very enterprising traders and handle the majority of grocery shops. They are not popular with the Egyptians, but seem to be tolerated. Said one man: "The Greeks are as prevalent and persistent as the flies"; and certainly nothing can stick like the Egyptian fly.

Dr. Quibel also commented favorably upon the native

[135]

industries, such as working in mother-of-pearl and ivory and small wood carving; beautiful fabrics in cotton, wool, and silk, both coarse and fine, made on hand looms, from the finest heavy silk weaves for scarfs and the satin striped goods for robes to the coarse cotton Turkish towelling; also the skilled working of brass, copper and metals, generally. These products I had already seen in the Cairo shops, as well as the working of leather, now going into the travelling bags and trunks, and some phonographic supplies, plumbing and heating articles, which are now being manufactured, but I confess these looked rather clumsy and primitive, though they are in vogue here, as the smart people who used to get all their sanitary arrangements from Europe, are encouraging the infant industry.

After a second round of coffee had been served, a party was assembled to visit the excavations—not far distant. Mr. Winlock explained that his system was to use native labour, men, women and children. They are divided into squads of ten with a "captain," and are paid a small pittance daily with a bonus of a certain percentage on the value of whatever the squad finds. This prevents a great deal of petty thieving and makes each worker a watcher of his neighbour, in whose find he shares—if it is duly turned in and credited to the squad. Every pinch of dust is fingered before being loaded into a small basket, which is carried a short distance and dumped into small flat cars, waiting to be filled, on narrow gauge rails. These are hauled away and "empties" take their places so long as the squads are working, usually about ten hours a day. Heat, and suffocating dust, which has lain for ages, and a rhythmic noise issuing from the throat of each worker, characterize the scene of labour. This noise, proved to be labour songs undulating in a short register, with interminable verses and repetitions, shrill and monotonous. They are led by a few of the older singers, and suggest the "Come-all-ye" of the Northwest, and the Canadian Chanty and the Sailor's "Heave-ho."

As nothing of importance was being unearthed for the moment, we soon left the stifling heat and dirt and made a start for Luxor, across the River several hours distant, and for the very welcome baths, clean linen and luxurious surroundings of the Winter Palace.

The next day at the French Consul's I encountered our host of the shared luncheon on the day before, the Sub-Mudir of Kenia. He was taking Oriental coffee with the Consul, as is the custom when any business is to be transacted, and a small brass tray on which was a tiny cup of thick black fluid was immediately brought for me. This was the opportunity to thank the Assistant Governor of the Province for his courtesy and, as he spoke English well, I was soon in possession of many interesting facts concerning the educational system of the Upper Nile; also his ideas of Egyptian social customs and the marriage laws which have been given under "The Other Woman and Her Education." He was full of offers to show me the various schools in Luxor.

None of this ever developed, however, for that evening I saw him at the Winter Palace in company with two American Ladies, whom I knew slightly, having been on the same steamer from New York, and who knew of my interest in the Egyptian women. This information had evidently been passed on. Oh, daughters of Eve, with the forked tongue! The gracious but courteous governor was lost to me.

His speech was most polite. He "regretted that it was not yet possible to arrange for the morrow to visit that school," but his eyes had the "Oriental look" and I knew he would be valueless to me. Evidently, he had been informed that I had been seeing Mme. Zaghlul Pasha and members of the Nationalist party, and, as he owes his job to English influence, he thought discretion the better part of . . . courtesy.

He was, without a doubt, right; and it was better so. The people themselves told me their story—from the Queen in Abdin Palace, through all the varying grades of Pashadom and the *Bourgeoisie,* down to the humblest *fellah* woman in her mud-hut—all were human documents, which gave the high lights of Modern Womanhood and her background, in this country whose history travels back 6,000 years to the borderland of fact and fiction—their belovèd Egypt.

BOOK II

ADVENTURING IN THE LAND OF AMMON-RA

CHAPTER XVII

ANIMALS AND THINGS, WISE AND OTHERWISE

COMING down to Cairo in the night train-deluxe from Luxor I met with an adventure that might have been draped with crêpe. Of course one may slip upon a banana skin—one of those small yellow ones so prevalent on the table d'hôte—and break one's back, but it is not usual. Neither is a scorpion landing in the middle of one's bed and disputing possession, a usual occurrence; but it can happen, and it did. Here is the story.

The continental sleeping-car has compartments like the staterooms in American cars which contain seats by day and metamorphose into beds by night. This compartment, for which I had expended much gold, had been built by a German firm for Egyptian travel, and had stamped plush panels, if you please, and a ceiling fresco of the goddess Isis, and the gods Horus and Anubis, very weird as to colour and drawing. As I was about to switch off the electric light and slip between the grey-looking sheets, my attention was arrested by this atrocious parody of an ancient art; or was it Anubis himself, the god of the underworld who had no wish to welcome me so soon to his domain and therefore held my hand suspended? At any rate, plump from the ceiling dropped an object upon my bed on the spot where another moment my shoulder would have been. It was a pale

[141]

stone-coloured beast about two inches long and built on the lines of a tiny lobster. As I gazed upon this object it suddenly doubled its tail to its head and proclaimed itself a scorpion and I waited for no further arguments. Snatching a towel I gave battle. Enveloping the creature within its folds, where it violently contorted in mad attempts to escape, I carried it to the window and sent it hurtling.

I was informed next day by a surgeon in Cairo that I should have sent for the guard, had the scorpion killed and the place searched for another, as the beasts usually go in pairs, and are not to be trifled with. The bite of a scorpion has often resulted in death in children or weak adults and in all cases the poison gives a very bad time. Whereupon I felt convicted of carelessness for the travelling public as this chap had evidently travelled a long way from the Sudan and doubtless had begun the journey very properly with his spouse.

Another excitement had been furnished the day before by the snake-charmer at Luxor. He was one of the Hawee, or snake players, who use, in their juggling tricks, the ancient Asp and the modern Nashir, a species of Cobra de capello (Coluber or Naja Haje), whose sacred name was Thermuthis. This very modern cobra was most well-behaved from a show-off standpoint. It stood up on its tail and flattened its head in a very good imitation of the bronze paper weight our loving friend brings home from Egypt. The day was a swirling hot one thrown into a group of windy, chilly, ones, and the cobra and the asp and a dozen or more snaky specimens, brought from the snake-charmer's basket, were very lively so that the man's stick was kept very busy con-

fining his wrigglers within a six-foot circle. Twice did
the asp and the cobra travel beyond bounds causing the
crowd of spectators, a group of tourists, to scatter. The
natives seemed to believe in these snakes for they took
no chances in allowing any to get near to them. It was
then that the asp invited me to do the Cleopatra act.
Absorbed in the strange power which the dusky, turbaned
Bedouin seemed to have over his cobra, I was roused by
my dragoman suddenly rushing forward and making a
few deft motions with his cane towards something at my
feet and the inquisitive asp, which in another instant
would have been sampling my ankle, was removed to a
safe distance near the feet of his charmer. It was not
my asp anyway. I have thought many pleasant things
about myself but never have got into the group of rein-
carnated Cleopatras.

"Madame must be careful," Shehata the dragoman
said gravely. "The snakes are not safe. They are not
doped and they have not their fangs removed and they
often bite Abdullah but the poison does not work on
him. He goes out on the desert and sings for a cobra
and when it comes he takes it and keeps it until it dies.
He cannot feed it, neither can he kill it, if he does either
of these things his power would go. When it dies he
goes into the desert and sings for another. The cobras
usually last about two weeks."

To be truthful, rather than romantic, I must confess
that the nearly-bitten thrills of asp and scorpion pale
into short lengths compared with that variety of Allah's
little creatures known as the flea. William Blake gave
the flea a soul, or at least drew a portrait of one. If the
Egyptian flea has a soul it is in charge of the Dark One.

[143]

A WOMAN TENDERFOOT IN EGYPT

It is both ubiquitous and venomous. It runs the Egyptian fly a close second, which is the worst reputation I can give it. If the glue manufacturers could separate and make use of the will to stick which animates every one of the millions of flies along the pleasant Nile there would be another group of pests removed from a land with tourists and money blest.

Another shadow streaking through one's pleasure, as one comes upon the gorgeous fields of poppies whose glorious great bells of mauve and white hang amidst the brilliant green of their luxuriant foliage, is the knowledge that they are grown not for their beauty but for the dreams at their heart. From them is made the native opium which is "bad, very bad for my people," says Shehata. These things, running like dark threads in a brilliant tapestry, only serve to accentuate the charm of this age-old land which lures with a thousand wiles the spirit of a modern Occidental.

While at Luxor we decided to visit what to my thought is the most fascinating Temple on the River—the one at Edfu. It meant an early uprising, which is a pleasure, rather than a hardship in this hot country.

With the chill of a desert wind searching one's marrow one feels like greeting the Sun God with praises and can realize how the deep religious fervor for the Sun could be built up in this country of contrasts and silhouettes; contrasts of heat and cold, light and dark. In the sun one is either blessèd warm or too hot, in the shade one is either blessèd cool or too cold—for the Gods can be cruel as well as kind.

Leaving Luxor at 6:20 A. M., I saw the Great God of the Sun, Ammon-Ra, slowly and majestically arise from his couch behind the Libyan hills and smile upon the green fields of the Nile belt. A fringe of acacia and fig trees outlined the squares of "grass," which is usually wheat or barley, and the alfalfa fields; then a village in a grove of date palms and surrounded by the usual irregular walls of mud bricks.

Of birds there were dainty little creatures, along the canals, which looked and acted like sandpipers; a fish-hawk flew by, and a large red-tailed hawk; a group of twenty Pelicans were posing on a sandy bar and occasionally I saw the ubiquitous English sparrow, probably a European import. The doves had long dark-grey tails, white underneath and rust-coloured bodies shading off into tan.

The Egyptian birds are astonishingly friendly. The doves alight on the balcony which one is also occupying, and the sparrows make free with room and chairs. I was startled from sleep one morning by a sparrow under the mosquito-netting, making me an involuntary hostess.

There were crows, grey and black, and vultures also. The goat and the sheep, that I saw in the fields were small with very long ears. The cow was the water-buffalo. The horses of Egypt are small also, except for an occasional Arabian beauty, and the donkey, long-suffering and mean-gaited, is at times incredibly tiny—a man's legs come within a few inches of the ground. Of course the camels are all very rangy and thin.

The second stop of the train was at Shagab. A youth in the long peasant *galabeyeh* of rusty black got on with his donkey and saddle. He was the sole occupant of a freight car open on the sides—which was attached in front of our car. Both he and the donkey stood up for two hours while the car bumped along, in dust and heat without apparently inconveniencing the youth any more than the donkey. It is this static animal-like acceptance of rigorous physical conditions, which to our more highly-civilized citizen would quickly produce fatigue, that I have often noticed in these children of much sand and little water.

The Libyan Range is on the east and the mountains of Matana back of the little town of that name. An hour's journey further on comes Esneh, with its Temple of the Ram-Headed God.

I noticed that the head of the Egyptian is always covered, while out-of-doors. Keep the back of the neck protected from the sun, is an axiom in the East. Even the children will have a sack thrown over the head and shoulders, if nothing else is available. One place we passed where trees were being planted. Deep pits had been dug and good earth brought to fill them. This was the method employed in the olden days to produce those beautiful avenues of green around the temples. Mr. H. E. Winlock, at Del-el-Beheri, had shown me such circles sixty feet in diameter in front of the Temple, near the tomb of Princess Nakt.

On the return trip from Edfu Temple we had a little experience with the ferry—now a modern boat with a spitting and fussy engine—which gives an idea of what this country was like before the Nile travel became standardized.

Before we left the west bank to return, Shehata, who was working for our interest, became involved in a violent lagomica, a veritable battle royal in guttural Arabic over the boat fare—sixty piastres was being charged us while other native passengers were paying ten. We had to prepare to leave his launch, a magnificent gesture as there was no other boat that would have connected with the train, before the boatman would consent to accept thirty piastres. Shehata said they are "very bad people," and had no fixed tariff, asking what they thought they could get. "Very bad people—there should be a tariff," he repeated.

"Why not complain to the Governor of the Province?" I asked.

"It should be done, but no one has thought it would be worth while. He is outside of the control," which meant license to commit any depredations that would be tolerated by the travelling public, the control being a British improvement.

Here should come a friendly warning to the enthusiastic investigator of foreign foods. A little strychnine is a good thing in the human body—more strychnine is a tragedy! Likewise the tall, upstanding sugar cane. It is succulent and nourishing and forms a staple article of diet for the lower classes of Egypt.

Moderation in eating is one of the first things the traveller must learn in any hot country, for the internal reactions are often sudden, surprising and painful. The delightful day's excursion from Luxor to the Temple of Edfu was capped by a two days' misery from over-indulgence in the sweet syrup that oozes from crushed sugar cane. There is no more agreeable way of crushing it, than to use the apparatus which nature has provided in one's twenty-four white grinders. My dragoman had a way of removing the outer layer, and cutting the cane into convenient lengths, which satisfied my hygienic scruples; and, as the day was hot and the bottled water exhausted, piece after piece of it was made to yield its sweetness and to go trickling down the "little red lane." By midnight the entire body politic was up in arms trying to conquer the intruder; relief parties had to be hastily organized and the devastated area was several days in recovering.

The moral of this little tale is not the badness of the sugar cane, but its goodness. In the George Ade vernacular it merely describes "The Good Sugar Cane and How She Got It Good."

In regard to this subject of food, the most delectable morsel that gladdened my palate in Egypt was the honey cake, a marvellous pastry of chopped almonds and honey coming originally from Syria. It was introduced to me by Mrs. Wm. duPont, who was presented by the stork to her parents while they were living in Syria and whose childish recollections held nothing so precious as this sweetmeat. It is beyond words enticing, but only the youthful digestion can afford to succumb to its charms.

Another gustatory memory is connected with the biblical pictures which are still being reproduced in the fields and along the canals of Egypt. The animals show up one by one instead of the two by two of Father Noah. One cow water-buffalo, flat head and angular legs, one donkey of the hee-hawing variety, one goat of rambumptious proclivities, one sheep, the brown woolly kind, and even one chicken, scrawny and athletic, will complete the group of samples. A *fellah* must be rich to have as many as those just enumerated. Usually the group consists of a sheep, a goat and either a donkey or water-buffalo. The milk of this last-named animal is widely used, but is rank in odour and taste. The goat's milk is much better. Never shall the memory die of an awful moment in the kitchen of a charming native hostess. I was invited to partake of some cheese made from the milk of the water-buffalo. A large wooden tub of it stood upon the tile floor and when the lid came off I realized the origin of the peculiar rancid odour that pervaded the room. My hostess not having a spoon handy swooped a large gob of the whitish compact mass upon her finger and offered it to me with the hospitable smile of a sweet and gracious woman at home. To refuse would have been an impossible breach of etiquette; so, a section of the cheese, shrieking malodorously to heaven, was transferred to my own finger, and, in the interests of friendship, the fell deed of eating it was consummated; and verily, like the small white globule with the slim green top which groweth in the garden of our own clime, the taste thereof abided for lo! a great number of hours.

CHAPTER XVIII

CARAVANING IN THE LIBYAN DESERT

I. THE START

WHEN the Poet and I decided to go camping in the Libyan Desert, we were not willing to wait a minute, and Shehata, the dragoman, agreed that he could be ready to start on the next afternoon. The Poet, a woman ridden by an ideal, which had led her into many strange places before this present plunge into the unknown, and I, a worshipper at the Shrine of the Out-of-Doors, packed our belongings with much glee and arranged to store the bulk of the luggage at Shepheard's Hotel, Cairo. As a precaution against being "murdered for the coral on our necks," I had given the dashing dragoman, whom we were trusting with our comfort and our lives, forty pounds in advance, and told him that no more would be forthcoming until our return to Shepheard's. The rest of our money and most of our jewelry, we locked up in the hotel safe. The manager looked astonished and disapproving, when I told him that if we were not back in a month it would be well to ask the American Consul to investigate. The few persons who knew that two women were starting off into the desert, alone with eleven black men, raised their voices in protest. But the adventure appealed to us, and one lovely evening early in March we piled our luggage into a mo-

[150]

CARAVANING

tor and merrily spun along the road to the Pyramids and the Meneh House.

The setting sun painted a brilliant orange background for the Pyramids, which, ever growing larger, as we approached, lured us like age-old beacons to a new life—new to us, but old, old as themselves, old almost, as the desert—the life of the Bedouin, of the free desert folk.

This is the Poet's reaction:

FREEDOM

Free as the coursing Arab rides my soul,
Out on the Desert far from all world stain,
Deep in my being lives triumphant pain,
All gained of love that indicates my goal.
My soul, up to the overturned bowl
That widens o'er, cerulean, it fain
Would reach some star-wrought height or
   God-built fane
To temples not of earth, to dwell, made whole
By love, oh soul that I adore, know me
And mark my soul, that ever rising, I
Will grow to blissful immortality!
Swim there with me through space, to glorify
Our souls— Ah, ride the Desert, lone, make free
With me, I'm only whole when Thou art nigh!
      Celia Louise Crittenton

Built on the edge of the desert, dominated by the Great Pyramid, the Meneh House combines the comforts of modern life with the joy of sand and sky. From private balconies one can watch the ever-changing lights on the huge triangle of Gizeh. Behind it the sunrise, the sunset,

A WOMAN TENDERFOOT IN EGYPT

the high noon and the high moon, the stars and fleecy clouds all play their part on the sky curtain of varying blue, from pale turquoise, from lapis-lazuli to sapphire. Who can describe its message? It beckons with a thousand fingers. It repels with a power dark, sinister, colossal, infinite. Men made it: and it sacrificed thousands and more thousands of them upon its stony form.

We had a quick dinner as we were keen to inspect our new quarters. Our caravan was encamped waiting for us almost at the foot of the eastern slope of the Great Pyramid. Against Shehata's advice I had ordered it placed there. I wanted to see the sun rise that way and capture the atmosphere of a bygone priestess of Ammon Ra, worshipping at the Temple of the Sphinx or, perhaps, to feel as the Poet did about it:

BEFORE THEE, OH SPHINX.

Could I remain near to Thee, shadowy Sphinx,
Though Thou dost smile, inscrutable, I feel
Some secrets I should win to make life real,
And add to time a few eternal links
That could support my soul before it sinks
To that new phase that no fled souls reveal.
Though time was short my passionate appeal
Gave back, from thy strange eye that winks
Not ever, though the human pests annoy,
An answer which was stirring to the part
Of me which is the Ever Me, and lo,
I knew! Oh, Face of Stone and Soul, destroy
Not my belief, just now, and kill my heart!
The secret lies with Us, oh Sphinx, till God
    say Yes or No!

[152]

CARAVANING

Like all cocksure persons I paid a heavy price for selecting this spot. When the first sun of our trip arose, I had no thought for the glories of antiquity, but was cursing the rascality of the present-day Arab. I had neither the jewels of the ancient religion nor the jewels on my fingers. Whom the gods seek to destroy they first make mad—there is no rational excuse for my leaving four valuable rings upon my fingers, nor finding it necessary to fasten my neck-wear with two large diamond pins. Having left all other valuables behind, in the pursuit of the simple life, why not these? And, having them, why not keep them on my person? But no, off came the diamonds and sapphires and pearls, just laid on the table at the head of my bed, beside a jewelled travelling clock. I had still many things to learn about commanding a caravan.

When we arrived at the spot where our Caravan was encamped, the Poet and I were delighted with the equipment. We had a gorgeous tent for dining, a cook tent and two bedroom tents. The inside of my tent was lined with an elaborate design of coloured linens with appliqué by hand. They were done in geometric patterns of flowers and leaves, and a border of Arabic letters, in white on a blue ground, contained mottoes from the Koran. Some of them were quaint indeed, when freely translated by Shehata:

"We all leave everything to God."
"Man has to be honest."
"We all have to be buried."
"When you do good you get it (good)."

There was also a very comfortable white iron bedstead, springs and mattress, a table, two chairs, a washstand and mirror, and a gorgeous thick-piled Oriental rug covered the canvas floor. The Poet's tent was similar. Her adventurous spirit however evaporated when she considered occupying it alone. So we decided to room together, and her bed was moved to the opposite side of my tent.

What a glorious night it was! The full moon touched all things with a resplendent glory. The floor of the desert looked black—glistening black—and the sky like a great over-bowl fitting tight down on the world rim, with Sirius, the evening star, Cassiopeia's chair, Vega and several of the planets shining fascinatingly near.

We retired early. A high desert wind flapped the tent walls incessantly. There were many strange noises about us, grunts of camels, snickers of donkeys, snores of men, snatches of guttural Arabic. Shehata had closed the flap of our tent and buttoned it down. The tent seemed stuffy and the flip-flop of canvas nerve-racking. It was not my idea of a good time. Not being able to undo the fastenings, I called to Shehata. He responded so suddenly that it made me jump. He was not a foot away—only the canvas wall between.

"Why, Shehata, what are you doing here?" I exclaimed. "You ought to have been in bed long ago." I had bade him good night an hour before. Gun in hand, he had announced that he would keep guard over us all night. He could trust his own people, he said. They were Bedouins —but the town Arab is a bad thieving rascal. Here by the Pyramids it was not safe. Out on the Desert it would be all right.

I had said "nonsense" and dismissed him.

He evidently had not gone, but had squatted on the sand at our door, gun on knees.

CARAVANING

I knew that Shehata had worked all the night before getting the caravan ready at very short notice and, indeed, had not had his clothes off, nor slept, for forty-eight hours. We of the Occident are not accustomed to that Spartan disregard of the body which these products of a more primitive age practise when occasion demands. It made me uncomfortable to have this man, already wearied in our service, pass another sleepless night in this silly business of guarding us. I not only insisted that he should retire but that the door of the tent should be left open.

He protested, I argued, and finally he acquiesced with dignity and said, "If Madame *commands* I must obey." "Very well, then," I said, feeling like a movie actress, "I command you to retire."

Even then, before leaving his post, Shehata installed a lieutenant in his place, with the gun.

The lieutenant squatted beside the partly open door, and promptly went to sleep. So did we—and the stage was properly set. Sometime before dawn, a little barefoot Arab had darted into our tent, past the sleeping Abdul-hadi, had grabbed the glittering clock and the glittering jewels, all nicely placed for him. He had also snatched up the Poet's shining bag, lying at the foot of her bed, and departed in the winking of an eye. When I awoke at sunrise my eyes blinked on a diamond bowknot pin lying on my chest. Evidently dropping it in his hurry the thief had not dared to return, and even so he might well be content with his booty. The Poet awaking at my exclamation, set up a wail at the loss of her bag and her toothbrush. Dressing quickly, I went forth and did a little woodcrafting which convinced me that none of my caravan was guilty. The tracks in the sand showed where the thief had sneaked along the canal, had made a quick dash in the open for our tent, which was the furthest removed from the rest of the caravan. His return tracks showed that he had sought the same cover. Not fifty yards away was the Poet's bag with all the articles intact except the soap and perfumery. It had been hurriedly inspected for valuables and, finding none, the rascal had been considerate enough to restore the, to him, useless, and, to the Poet, most necessary, articles of toilet.

Shehata, now coming up and hearing of the robbery, took it like a Bedouin. He offered no word of reproach for my commanding him to retire the night before, but prostrating himself in the sand began to kiss my feet and to pray. Another most uncomfortable moment—very embarrassing to have one's feet kissed by six feet of lordly male, all resplendent in satin and silk, and with an immortal soul besides. I finally had to do the movie stunt again and "commanded" him to rise and stop praying and discuss the matter. We decided to send a messenger at once to the Gizeh Police Station to report the theft. Then to have breakfast, after which "Madame had best go to the station herself and lodge a complaint and arrange to have the pawn shops of Cairo notified."

After breakfast, which we enjoyed—for I had concluded that when one begged to be robbed as I had, one might as well take it philosophically—I decided to go on with the trip, having convinced myself that Shehata was in no way responsible for the robbery. The caravan was being struck, and I told Shehata that it was

[156]

a good time to go to the Police Station. He bowed but made no move. I wondered what was the matter now, and was soon enlightened. Coming across the desert was a group of camels and Arabian horses galloping madly towards us.

"If Madame will deign to wait. Some of my people are coming." Madame must perforce wait, as, one by one, throwing themselves out of their saddles, the male relatives of Shehata approached and lined up before me, while Shehata prostrated himself, as before, in the sand at my feet. There were five husky Bedouins of the Nagama tribe in rich robes of striped satin, of pongee and of heavy broadcloth, embroidered. Two uncles and cousins of varying degree, all occupying honourable positions in their tribe. The big, dignified uncle Abdul Mahamet Taleb, who had been Maude Adams' dragoman, was presented and began an eloquent plea for Shehata.

"He is a good boy. He never drinks. He is kind to his children. He stands by his friends. He is absolutely honest. We are all honest, but it has been remarked that Shehata is more careful than we. He comes from an honourable family. His disgrace will be our disgrace. He is a good dragoman. He has been trained by myself and his maternal uncle," waving a hand towards a tall, straight man in blue broadcloth and turban. "You will find that he will do everything possible to serve you."

The maternal uncle, a most honourable Emdeh, head Sheikh of Sheikhs, now placed his hand upon Shehata's shoulder and said in broken English: "Shehata is my child. He is good. He would do no harm."

[157]

The three big cousins nodded approvingly. I bowed to the honourable deputation and enquired: "Shehata, what is it all about?"

"If Madame makes a complaint at the Police Station, Shehata will be put in jail and my people will be disgraced."

A great light dawned.

"Tell these honourable gentlemen that I believe you to be honest and that you had no part in the robbery. Indeed, you did everything you could to prevent it. And that when I go to the Police Station I shall lodge no complaint against you."

This news was received with satisfaction. Shehata was embraced by each relative in turn, and the cavalcade departed in a flurry of flying heels.

Crime, or accusation, defence, retribution, follow fast in the desert. The clan feeling is as strong as it was on the Scottish Border in days gone by. The matter of saving Shehata had been dealt with at once by the quick action of brain and brawn rather than by the slow grinding mill of the Law.

Even the most sanguine caravaner will have to admit that this was not an ideal start. However, being now, as it were, stripped for action, relieved of my dangerous wealth by foul means, since I had not been possessed of enough wisdom to dispose of it by fair means, we were ready to plunge into the desert and the unknown.

The Poet elected to begin her adventures with an overbrimming cup and was hoisted on to Adelia, a temperamental riding dromedary, who received her burden with sniffs of comment far from complimentary. Her "boy," Abdul, aged sixty, whispered into Adelia's left ear, no

CARAVANING

doubt a promise that Allah would reward her in camel paradise, and she subsided. The Poet wabbled and clutched. Adelia sidestepped and lurched. My donkey, George Washington, took a dozen steps to Adelia's one. And I looked like a Harbor tug beside an Ocean Liner. Shehata, ever near, swung his long legs over the back of a diminutive donkey with incredible pipe-stem legs. Abraham Lincoln was his name for a moment. He had been Grover Cleveland, President Wilson, "Teddy" Roosevelt, in turn, according to his "boy's" idea of the mood, or politics, of the American customer who would pay good backsheesh for being carried on him. His grey coat with a few black stripes, suggestive of a zebra, on the haunches, was close-clipped. The mane was roached, the tail hair cut squarely off and a red ribbon braided in it. Tinkling little bells had been clamped into his ear tips. A grey headnet of open-work chenille, a fancy leather saddle with red and blue morocco-leather trimmings, and an Oriental rug under it all, showed "Abe" to have fallen upon pleasant places and the happy possessor of a donkey boy of parts. All this gorgeousness had been designed for "Madame," but a short trial convinced Madame that some of the tricks of Mohamet the "boy," were not to her liking. The ever-active stick, which all the donkey boys carry, the playful habit of twisting Abraham Lincoln's tail at unexpected moments, Abe's own acrobatic method of relieving himself of the attentions of embarrassing flies, and above all the loud and persistent vocalizations of Mohamet, a smiling devil of nineteen, resulted in Madame's decision to ride the beast which Shehata had picked out for himself—just a "very good donkey."

A WOMAN TENDERFOOT IN EGYPT

The Sun was high in the Heavens, its fierceness tempered by the desert wind.

Behind us, the caravan ambled single file at a three-mile-an-hour gait. I looked back and felt a thrill of pride that this shaky, undulating line of camels, carrying loads like young houses, and responding to the will of the driver, belonged to me. I could stop them when I liked and I could travel them hard, or easy, and go where I liked. So long as the gold held out, I was queen of nine camels, one riding dromedary, three donkeys and eleven black men. Food there was, and tents and comforts—yes luxuries—all in my little kingdom.

The long hours of the march were spent, usually, riding at the head of the caravan as we travelled, what to me, was a pathless waste of ever-changing perspectives; for the desert is not flat, really. It is constantly being milled into little hills and valleys by the wind and at times violently changed by the simoon and the sirocco. A hundred feet sometimes would completely hide from view our slow-plodding beasts and the creature comforts they represented. Sometimes we rode at the end of the caravan so as to avoid any possibilities of losing it, as our little party of the Poet on her Adelia, and Shehata and "Madame" on donkeys, was more mobile than the string of pack camels, which, once loaded and started must be kept in motion, steady and slow, the tortoise trail. A loaded camel, stopped, will lie down and loosen the load. A running, or galloping, camel will soon have his burden strewed on the desert sands. The camel's principal food

CARAVANING

is clover, and he is a cunning beast, having many trade tricks for making the burdens imposed upon him by man more tolerable. When the saddle is being put on, he will swell his barrel so that the girth, later, will be useless as a cinch. The packers know this, as well as the vigorous protests a camel makes while being loaded. He will squeal and grunt in apparent agony as each new weight is added to the pile, until a surprising amount of stuff is accumulated. To one accustomed to the Rocky Mountain pack train and the carrying capacity of a horse, the camel load seems appalling. The humane maximum for a horse on level ground is two hundred pounds. Our camel carried four or five times that weight. Iron bedsteads, chairs, chest of drawers, washstand, tables, besides baggage rolls and boxes were piled on him. Baskets, bags and packages of every description were massed on top of that load, until nothing showed but his ungainly legs with their large padded feet, his restless, ratty tail and a long neck, arching and curving, as it carried the all-important engine of this body-economic which has made the camel as a beast of burden, from time immemorial, useful to man. The camel's head is small, its jaw undershot, armed with powerful teeth which are no mean weapons of defence. The hospitals always have some cases of camel-bites, sometimes serious ones. The camel's eyes are small and rarely friendly. When he is being loaded, his eyes are vicious and snappy, and why not? Are they not the windows of the soul? At any rate, of the brain, whose will has been bent to man's will. The camel resents this with all a slave's cunning and ferocity. That is the rebellious engine driving this incredible ship of the desert which requires so little fuel, so little stoking and watering on the long, weary, marches over the biggest, most inhospitable spaces on the earth's surface.

The dromedary is a smaller, more highly-specialized animal. He will not carry heavy loads, has an easier gait than the camel; and a riding dromedary, like Adelia, means one that has been especially selected for its gait, and trained to respond to certain pressures and sounds and produce a walk, a canter—which is the easiest gait—a slow run, a fast run. It also throws in, without training, and, if angry, certain side steps and jumps, a spurt forward and a sudden stop and a series of acrobatic feats uncommonly like a bronco's bucking—all of which is calculated to unseat any but the most skilful rider.

I shall never forget an exhibition which Adelia gave one day when we were taking a side excursion from the Pyramids to the Petrified Forest. As it was not a long trip, the Poet had elected to ride George Washington, who laid back his ears in disgust when the accustomed weight of his rider proved to be considerably augmented. Adelia had obediently knelt down and allowed me to settle comfortably upon her luxurious saddle, which was covered with an Oriental rug of silky softness, and ornamented with embroidered saddle-bags with much knotted and befringed worsted of bright colours. She wore several necklaces of coloured beads and a string of little bells given to her by previous admirers. Her head was covered with bright worsted fly-net with silver ornaments. Very smart indeed was Adelia, and all went well for the first mile. Then, contrary to custom, Abdul, the sixty-year-old "boy" of Adelia, was sent

[162]

back on an errand and we proceeded without him. The donkey boys had also been left behind.

Adelia endured the desertion of her Abdul for a time, doubtless expecting him to return. Then her outraged dignity began to mount, and she grew peevish. She would not canter, but used her hardest walk, then a short hard trot. She was not trying to throw me, only to be disagreeable. Occasionally she told me what she thought about it in a low snarl. Her ears were slanted back "cross," not vicious. Then they would have been laid flat back. Her eyes had a nasty gleam. Her usual rider was missing and the usual weight, and Abdul gone. Something was wrong. Being temperamental she grew more and more nervous and fidgety and so did the female on her back. When we dismounted at the Petrified Forest I decided that the Queen of the Caravan and her nervous subject had parted company for that day. It looked as though it would be a case of "Willy come here," "Well Willy, don't come here. You shall mind." To avoid any risk of *lése majesté* I firmly mounted "Abe" Lincoln and left Adelia to the lordly Shehata. Then the circus began, a one ring, but replete with excitement and variety.

This desert-trained Bedouin, annoyed that Madame should have been annoyed, undertook to show Adelia "what's what." And Adelia resented the Master's touch and the disciplining hand—resented it in every quivering fibre down to her toes, her tail tip and her teeth. Snarling and squealing with rage she dashed away at her fastest run, twisting, turning, jumping and stopping short; then dashing on again. None but an athlete, born to the

[163]

job, could have stayed on that gyrating perch. I would have been off at a tangent on the trail to China at the first demi-volt. But stay on he did, and mercilessly he belaboured her and bent her will to his, this master of the Desert children. In a quarter of an hour, a quivering, foam-flecked, sweat-soaked and dejected Adelia, consented to amble quietly beside us on the return journey.

In a short time Shehata asked permission to halt our procession. He dismounted, and, having nothing else available, he sacrificed an extra scarf he was wearing as a sash, and rubbed down Adelia. This Captain of the Caravan who never did a stroke of manual labour in the presence of his men, now went over the dripping Adelia, dried her off, restored her coat to glossy smoothness, wiped her face, her eyes and behind her ears. He worked quickly, but thoroughly. He readjusted her trappings, mended a broken strap and I remounted a rejuvenated, but chastened Adelia.

It is a strange blend, this desert fierceness and gentleness. The sharp agony of the simoon and the cool refreshment of the oasis are blended in the nature of the Bedouin. Cruel as Hell, gentle as Heaven.

3. PRINCESS NEB

In the Cairo Museum I had seen the jewels of Princess Neb-Hetepti-Khrot found at Dashur by de Morgan in 1894. There was a beautiful silver diadem inlaid with stones and the Uraeus-Serpent of royalty in front; necklaces and bracelets for her fair throat and arms: parts of a fan, set in semi-precious stones—with what effect she must have coquetted with it—and, intriguing thought, a

[164]

gold dagger-blade! Jewels, a crown, a fan, a dagger and a tomb, is all that is left to reconstruct the vivid life of a Princess of the 12th Dynasty, when Sebek-Nofru, the Great Queen, held her sway—2000 to 1788 B. C. It was an epoch of great buildings of Egypt's most prosperous activity. Art and Literature flourished and the workers in precious metal were at their best.

On the edge of the Desert stand the Pyramids of Dashur. They were our immediate objective, and the second night found us encamped within a few miles of them. In the early morning, while the caravan was being assembled and packed for the day's march, we trotted straight in the face of the mounting sun, passed the Blunted Pyramid of Dashur, and on to the South Brick Pyramid. It was built, the antiquarian says, by King Amenemhit III. It used to be covered with limestone slabs. Having already absorbed our impressions of Sakkara, its Step Pyramid, its Serapeum, or Tomb of the Sacred Bulls, and the other tombs and pyramids of that group, some of which were visible at a distance, this Brick Pyramid held us but a short time. The Poet pined to get the "atmosphere" of the Princess with the consonanted name, so we continued a little to the north, where, enclosed by a former girdle-wall, was the last resting place of Princess Neb-Hetepti-Khrot.

There was little to see when we got there, just the "usual tomb chamber and passages," said the Poet resignedly.

"Why cannot these discoverers leave their discoveries, instead of scattering their remains all over the civilized globe! Even the old Bulls in the Serapeum had to go travelling."

[165]

A WOMAN TENDERFOOT IN EGYPT

She was remembering our visit to Sakkara the week before, when a friend's motor car had transported us over precarious wheel ways along canals to Bedrashein. These camel and donkey paths are the only motor roads available, outside of the big cities. At Bedrashein, the dragoman and donkeys had awaited us, and the party had started towards Memphis with the usual racket. We had seen the usual sights which every Egyptian tourist never fails to see, with the additional spice of being allowed to go inside of the working enclosure of an excavating party. We had seen the skulls and hands and feet of mummies sticking out of the hillside and had examined many pieces of rare pottery, piled up for classification and ultimate delivery to Museums.

"It is an age of exploitation and utilitarianism." (The Poet never hesitated to use long words.) "Those poor mummies over there in the Seti burial ground," she nodded towards Sakkara, "have gotten away with it for thousands of years, and now, because there is so much money in the pockets of a few fools that they do not object to spending some of it, this company of the dead must be routed out of their peace and made to furnish a passing show for the giggling school child of today."

It was a pretty speech. I attempted to appease the Parnassian wrath. "Too bad Princess Nibs did not yield anything exciting in her tomb, but she probably feels worse about it than we do. She would have liked to have been depicted in her best clothes, like those white flowing gauze garments of Queen Nefekket up at Luxor with her most charming *lavallière* and necklaces and bracelets. But the lovely Nefekket was a Queen, wife of Rameses II., while Neb-H. K. here was only a princess,

[166]

probably the fourth daughter of the fourth wife of her father."

The Poet looked at me pityingly. "You know those old boys did not have four wives at a time, that was a Moslem trick. Your data is all wrong. Those ancient kings had only one wife at a time. They just strangled or drowned or poisoned a wife when she became inconvenient. Unless she beat him to it. Cleopatra, and her three predecessor Cleopatras, all seemed to be efficient at the murder game."

"*Allons*," said I, speaking a foreign language to impress the Poet with the fact that I , too, knew something. "*Allons*, I see the sha-a-dow (the Poet's name for the ever-present Shehata) is approaching. The sun is half way to high noon, which means the caravan is already started and we must travel to overtake it."

.

4. THE DESERT

There is a lure in the Desert life that I have felt nowhere else to so great a degree. The majestic friendship of the vast mountains that companion the sky and freely offer shelter, warmth and food for the knowing one who has heard the "Red God's Call," puts the soul upon stilts in order to measure up to its grandeur. But the Desert demands a different kind of hardihood, a different courage, or approach, to its infinite spaces. One must have the sagacity of the serpent for its fiercer moods, the gentleness of the dove for its tender moments. Man's brain must provide the needs for man's body. The Desert yields him nothing but light and air, and showers these blessings at times in such titanic quantities that finite man is well-nigh overwhelmed. In its gentler moods, the Desert achieves the sunrise and the sunset and she ever lingers softly near the green fronds of the date palms and the sparkling jewels of the Water God, who dwells in every well and tiny waterway.

On the third morning of our march Shehata, by my order, scratched on the tent outside my bed at about five o'clock. The signal was sufficient to awake me but not to disturb the Poet, whose great charm was that she did not always want to do what I did. Hastily getting into proper footwear, winding a rose chiffon veil, turban fashion, over tumbled hair and throwing a long coral cloak about me, I prepared to greet the Sun God. Stepping from our tent, which was always set facing the East, the dawn wind greeted me, sharply sweet. The camp was deserted, sleeping, save for Shehata who hovered near— not too near. My business was with the Great God Ammon-Ra, Lord of the Sun, whose glorious smile was just appearing on the horizon. The great golden disc, blazing six times the splendour of that orb when it rises over the lake in far-off Connecticut, blinded me with the glitter of its energy. It was the time of the "big sun" as well as the "big moon" and no human eye can gaze into it with safety. Turning a little, there grew upon me, attuned to one of the Desert's great moments, a vision of rare beauty. We had camped on the edge of a small oasis. Before me in a grove of date palms was a well and a *shaduf*, that simple device for lifting water from the well into the irrigation ditches that had created this paradise. Two young men of magnificent proportions, naked save for a breech cloth, were assisting the Water God in his beneficent offices. Their pale brown bodies were

[168]

CARAVANING

dripping with water and sparkling off in a thousand drops,
as the muscles played under the glistening skin and,
touched by the rising sun, shone like living bronze statues.
They embodied the charm of peaceful occupation bro-
thered to the Desert. That scene, by turning the reel
of time backward, has been enacted daily even as the sun
has poured his glance upon it for unnumbered years,
reaching back farther and farther into the unwritten an-
nals of sand and water.

5. FATIMA THE JESTER

Slipping into the tent, I wooed another hour of obliv-
ion. Then came a bath in a rubber tub and a delicious
breakfast by François, our cook. François was the
blackest black man I have ever seen, a Sudanese who had
been trained in the culinary art by a Frenchman.
Blessed be his name! He was a true *cordon bleu*. No
wielder of the pot and skillet ever produced more
delectable results than our François. And, as Shehata manœuvred with much adroitness to obtain fresh
vegetables and chickens and eggs, our table was a joy
and a constant surprise.

If we were within possible distance, swift runners were
sent out the night before, whose mission it was to bring
in the next morning's fresh supplies. We were not conscious of the technique, but the delicious, well-served
meals in those barren wastes of sand and sky served to
furnish another contrast for our growing collection. My
memory of the cook is always climaxed by an amusing
incident that happened a few days out.

The caravan was well started. Adelia and her Poet

were at the head of it. A loosened girth had caused me to drop behind, while Shehata fixed it. As our donkey gait was faster than the camel pace, we were slowly catching up to the long sinuous line of the camels with their huge loads and faithful "boys." It ever fascinated me. Soon my eye was attracted by the last but one, known as the Cook's Camel. It was always the last to be packed and the first to be unpacked and always on the top was to be found the Cook, himself. His fat unwieldy body never made the long marches on foot. In reverence to his office, and perhaps to his necessity, François sat upon his throne of pots and pans like an Oriental potentate upon his palanquin.

The Cook's Camel was behaving strangely, though no one seemed to notice it. She—of course the cleverest of the lot were shes—was stepping very gingerly—a slow, smooth tread. She equalized the unevenness of the Desert floor by long or short steps, so that that load remained poised, as nearly stationary as possible. The Cook, lulled by this peace, dozed placidly. Her boy dozed as he plodded alongside, when suddenly the miracle happened and all was explained. With one mighty lunge forward, Fatima stepped clean from under her load and like Humpty Dumpty, down came kettles and stoves and Cook and all. That foxy Fatima had realized that her fastenings were insecure and had manœuvred until she had cleared herself entirely, then, choosing the right moment, had made this *coup* with complete success. She turned and ambled past us, and if ever a camel laughed, she was doing it. I laughed back in her face as she went by.

A moment's stunned silence, and pandemonium broke

CARAVANING

loose. Every camel-boy, every donkey-boy, broke forth
into the violent gutturals of their pet "cuss words" mixed
with orders wildly given. Orders to catch Fatima, to
keep the other camels from lying down, or stampeding, or
otherwise upsetting their loads. Shehata and I rushed to
Mr. Dido in the ruins of his kingdom. Fortunately
nothing was cracked, but his dignity, his bulk having
managed to land on top of the stove instead of under it,
and his laments rose in high squeals over the general cho-
rus. How anything short of a hundred throats could
have produced such a volume of sound would surprise any
one who is not accustomed to the Arab chattering.
Vocalization seems to be a mental safety valve. For
twenty minutes the babel continued until the unrepen-
tant trickster, Fatima, was captured and reloaded and
the Cook, with Spartan courage, again enthroned upon
her.

6. DONKEYS, SAND FORTUNES AND OATHS

The Donkeys were curious little beasts with distinct
personalities. Shehata's long legs when stretched out,
while riding "Abe" Lincoln, came within a foot of the
ground. Many a race we had to enliven the long march,
and, occasionally, when the shifting sand made foothold
treacherous, my donkey, or his, would go tumbling head
over heels. One had such a little way to go that the spill
was never bad. Also on the long marches, whenever
the mobile wing of the caravan halted for a picnic lunch
or a side trip of sightseeing, Abdul would be pressed into
service to tell our fortune in the sand. He always carried
his equipment for this in a bandanna handkerchief, tucked

somewhere in the trappings of Adelia. More often than not, the Poet would be seated upon her temperamental transportation, and the squares would be drawn large in the sand so that they easily could be seen. Pebbles, a certain number in each square, following some ritualistic ceremony of Abdul's, would be juggled according to a formula, and then Abdul was ready—as soon as his "palm had been crossed with silver." The spell never worked without that part of the entertainment. With that prescience so common in the East, Abdul often gave forth oracular utterances. When halted by lack of inspiration or English—for of this he had only a meagre quantity—he would fall back on his stock phrase, which was, "Dis is all the dissert." With a grandiloquent gesture he said this a dozen times a day, and a more or less toothless, but engaging smile, captivated one into receiving this startling intelligence as though it had burst forth for the first time. Many fortune-tellers have told me stories in the sand, by the hand, and by "the stars." None was cleverer than Abdul-ha-di, but that is not saying very much. If there are any really good exponents left of the ancient art of the Seers, I have not been fortunate enough to find them.

He also enlightened me on the subject of Oaths. There are Oaths, and Oaths—well, not so binding, such as *Allah, Allah By the Koran, By the first divorce,* etc. But, when a man swears,

> *Telakh bi te-la ta*
> *By the Third Divorce*

there is no going back on that, as a man cannot divorce a third time and marry again. Then, Shehata contributed the following legend to point this sad moral!

"A caliph had a favourite wife who was very aggravating. He divorced her for the third time. Then realizing what he had done, he sent for his wise men. They said, 'It is finished.' The caliph said, 'You better reconsider, or your heads may be finished.' So they married her to a pool of water, put her in it; and then the Caliph took her back."

7. THE DESERT'S FIERCER MOOD—THE SIMOON

That night we were far in the Desert on the trail to the Fayum, and the Poet and I were caught in the grasp of one of the Desert's fiercer moods—a simoon. It happened at night. We had made camp late, owing to the delay caused by our vaudevillian Fatima in the morning, and to the need of making half-way to an oasis we hoped could be reached by the following night. The wind was high and blowing occasionally fine sand-showers upon us as we sat in our steamer chairs after dinner enjoying coffee and the usual glorious sunset. It was wonderful that evening but with a new colour note in it, a blurring of the orange and a sharpening of the violets—a distinct purple haze. Shehata knew, but he said not a word. In the East, one does not anticipate trouble. "Never trouble trouble till trouble troubles you," an excellent adage which the animals and some Orientals have not as yet unlearned.

There was a sense of nervousness and unrest in the air and the gusty wind was hot. Shehata looked at the southern and the eastern sky.

"Would the ladies like to have their chairs in the tent?"

[173]

he questioned. The feverish wind was flapping our garments and the fine sand occasionally stung against our cheeks. Yes, the ladies would. It was not the moment to read, to play cards,—even, to talk, and, as for communing with the Desert night, this wild unfriendly thing that stalked abroad would brook no communing. Even the night's children were veiled from us. The friendly low-hung sociable stars were gone. We decided to go to bed. The last retiring ceremony was always adjusting the door flap for air. When the Poet was tucked snugly between the sheets of her comfortable single bed on one side of the tent and mine was waiting invitingly for me on the other side, she would put out the light and I would button the flap half-way and place a chair, covered with a rug, in the opening. This served to protect us from inquisitive eyes, although our tent was always placed on the edge of the encampment, and from intrusion by prowling desert beasts, jackals, perhaps, or a desperate hyena. So Shehata said. Personally, I never believed that any wild animal would venture so near the human smell in a human den, as it were. However this was a compromise, as Shehata had tried from the first to keep our door flap closed at night.

On this growling, snarling night Shehata was firm. "Madame will please keep her tent closed tonight. The wind is high."

Though disposed to rebel and not knowing what he knew, that soon a little group of human maggots would be swept over by a mighty power that counted them as naught, I remembered the first night when my pigheadedness produced such sad results and meekly closed the flap. I heard it being buttoned down tightly. Then I

[174]

heard thump, thump, thump, and knew that our tent
stakes were being driven yet more firmly into the sand;
and then, that small rocks were being piled around each
stake. I could hear above the incessant flapping of our
canvas walls, the firm tones of Shehata giving orders.

I must have dozed a little, as one might in a boiler fac-
tory. The continual racket of the wind tearing at our
tent was soporific. I was startled to sharp wakefulness
by a hand grasping the bedclothes and shaking them.
Incidentally it had also grasped my foot. It was attached
to Shehata, who, still outside the tent, had been trying in
vain to rouse me by voice.

"Madame, it is come." He shouted. "You will be
safe. Madame will please wrap up warm and lie on the
rug under her bed, and lie still, no matter what happens."
The Poet had no need to be told. We hastily wrapped
ourselves like cocoons under our beds and with a terrific
roar the simoon was upon us. Another tearing, thudding
noise punctuated the uproar. It was the dining room
tent blown down, and a crash of crockery and glass. The
other tents had gone before. Our tent still stood by virtue of every stake being manned by a human body lying
on the guy ropes and tamping, tamping into the sand its
particular stake. Fine sand was forced through our canvas walls in waves, forced through two thicknesses of
heavy canvas and an inner lining of tight-weave cotton.
Even the heavy Oriental rug, where it was not held down
by furniture and our bodies, billowed with the wind seep-
ing under it.

Any instant the tent might go. Thus we went on
through the night. How long I know not. Often I went
blurring off into blankness, always to find, upon coming

up to the surface of consciousness, that the tamp, tamp, tamp of our faithful men was keeping our desert roof over our heads.

At dawn the fury had past, the rescue work was over and the camp was sleeping. The animals still crouched flat tails to the wind in terror-stricken exhaustion. Only the ever-watchful Shehata was awake. I commanded him to retire, and he went. The Desert was smiling again with the sunrise. The Poet and I scraped the sand off our mattresses and laid ourselves upon them. It may be we said a little prayer before we slept.

8. THE BEDOUIN WEDDING

Events were crowding now. We pushed on that day, as planned, for there was to be a Bedouin "Wedding" of a real Desert Tribe that night at the Oasis near which we expected to camp. It was a hard day. Every one was jaded, but no murmur of protest reached me. All the caravan were eager for the new excitement.

The Desert was especially sweet that day with many a little hill and dale new-put by the master mason of the night before. A gentle breeze tempered the tropic sun. About five o'clock we made camp. An early dinner and then for the Bedouin festivity. All kinds of festivities are called "Weddings." No one was really getting married on this occasion but it was some minor Mohammedan feast day. A nomadic tribe of the North African Berbers, those inheritors of the fiery blood of their forefathers who achieved such marvellous exploits under the banner of the Prophet, had joined forces with a tribe settled in this Oasis to make a "party." I was keen to

[176]

see so typical a Bedouin performance. As at the time of Herodotus the tent of the true Bedouin is still his home. But the Poet was tired. She did not share my ethnological enthusiasm to the extent of further effort that night. I decided to go alone and to leave Shehata in charge of the Poet and the camp. This idea was violently opposed, especially by Shehata who said he would trust Madame with no one but himself.

As usual, we compromised. Shehata was to take me there, for I had begun to learn that when he insisted, there was usually, like a certain cereal, a reason. Then Gameel, the husky son of the Sheikh of Abuskir who was acting as "boy" to "Abe" Lincoln was to take me home, which would permit Shehata to return to camp earlier.

This program was carried out, with the exciting results that I am about to relate.

Shehata and I started off alone across the trackless waste as the last brilliance of the afterglow was fading into the deep blue-black curtain of a moonless night. The stars slipped out one by one. In three minutes the camp had vanished like a spent reel. We had about four miles to go; no distance at all on a charted path. It might have been the whole of the Sahara so far as my ability to find either the camp or the oasis went. I was absolutely dependent upon this man to guide me. It was rather a curious sensation. An expression upon the Bedouin's face told me that his thoughts were far from peaceful, that he was not concerning himself with the beauty of the night. But I was not alarmed. I had already established supremacy over the Captain of our Caravan and I knew also, that all his interests lay in serving me well. For this he would get much gold and much reputation, and many new customers. The Dragoman has a character to sustain. Also there was that little matter of the robbery. He must continue to demonstrate that it was not his fault, and to live up to the high recommendations of his male relatives. I soon forgot him. The lure of the Desert was pervasive, languorous. The wanton night was in a most provocative mood. It made one lonesome, an urge to share its beauty. What a night for lovers!

It was a fitting preparation for the wild scene which was rolled before me that night. In half an hour we were skirting the edge of the little fertile ravine, and the noise of many voices, rising rhythmically, and shot through with shouts and the occasional report of a revolver, made us realize that the "wedding" was already in full swing.

The moon now leisurely turned on her spot-light, and I saw the central figure of this kaleidoscope, a native dancing girl, a *ghaziyeh,* in voluminous flounced skirts and tight basque of coloured calico. Her waist was cut in by a narrow, tight belt, which further emphasized the curving lines of her very full bust and hips. The slender arms were bare and covered with gold junk, bracelets, bangles, chains. The face was uncovered, but a gauzy veil floated on the head and was used for posturing. Her well-shaped feet and ankles were bare. Glimpses of silver anklets and hennaed toes and heels were given, as her feet twinkled in and out under the long skirts. She was surrounded by a quadruple circle of men, perhaps 200, mostly in the white woollen bournouse with the pointed hood of the Bedouin. They were beating time for her

[178]

dancing, by clapping hands and knees rhythmically, and chanting a loud call which gathered volume until the air throbbed with it. Then, diminishing, till a lower note was reached, when the notes swelled again. It was a great urge from each man to become the favoured suitor of the *ghaziyeh*—for that brief hour queen of all—while she danced faster and faster, hesitating only till she should decide which of the gallants should be her choice. At each new round, her gestures and postures became more provocative, until she threw her veil over a handsome youth in the violently pleading circle. He instantly seized her, swung her from the ground and carried her away, out of the circle into the night.

The ring did not break up but another dance girl appeared and the love game went on. It was frankly a sex dance and the mass psychology was frankly that. No one could remain unconscious of it.

With the exception of the girl gesturing her suggestive dance in the arena of chanting males, I was the only woman present.

"Where are the women?" I asked of Shehata who was guarding me closely, an anxious look chasing after an excited one, like flying clouds in a "mackerel sky."

"Oh, Madame, they are in the women's quarters. You can hear them over there," pointing to a quadrangle of thatched shelters and tents. The tinkle of singing and laughter floated to us, and the sounds of native music. The thum of the *darabukeh,* a native drum, and the rattle of the *nakkarah,* a semi-spherical tambourine.

"N-i-c-e women do not come to this part of the "wedding." With you it is different. Every one knows Madame is a great American Lady. She can do as she likes." Shehata gave an expressive shrug. "Over there is the Emdeh, the Sheikh of Sheikhs, of the Great Utad Ali Tribe, a very great man. Would Madame like to meet him?"

Just then several volleys of revolver shots, fired presumably in the air, but very erratically pointed, decided me that a greater distance from the madly-excited revellers might be advisable. We moved a hundred paces or more to where a small crowd of men were grouped about the very commanding figure of the Emdeh, a man perhaps of forty with piercing black eyes and full beard and moustache, robed in white woollen *galabeyeh* and gorgeous striped satin under robes. The jewelled hilt of a dagger showed in his silken sash.

The crowd made way for us respectfully. Shehata made quite a little speech in Arabic introducing the "American Lady who was a great Sheikh among women in her country." The Emdeh acknowledged this flamboyance with flashing approving eyes and bowed. Then, horror of horrors, I committed a breach of etiquette, unpardonable, without precedent. I offered my right hand, in the ordinary act of courtesy, to shake hands with the Emdeh. There was a moment of stunned silence. I heard Shehata murmur in English: "My God, Madame, what are you doing?"

The Emdeh took a step forward, swept back his robes from a muscular hand and with a magnificent gesture grasped my little flipper. Suddenly he seemed to tower over me and around me. I was surrounded by satins and silks and sandal wood odours. I stiffened with fear, remembering that to the Bedouins in that encampment, the Emdeh's power is supreme.

[180]

CARAVANING

"Shehata, tell him that in my country shaking hands is a mark of respect among equals," I wafted hurriedly out of the draperies.

Shehata fairly sputtered Arabic in getting this out. There was a moment's hesitation. The satin chest rose in a mighty breath—and fell. The powerful hand sent a wave of energy through mine. I felt the whole wild spirit of the East surge around me,—and surge back again. Then the enveloping robes of the Emdeh fell away from my small person. He stepped back with much dignity, bowed and said, "Madame, does me much honour."

"Madame, it would be wise to get out of this," Shehata's face was chalky white. "I did wrong to bring you here, Madame has been too gracious. The Bedouin women do not behave thus, unless they are willing to give favours. The Emdeh may prevent your leaving. In that case I may not be able to help it. Do not appear to hurry, but edge out of the crowd till I can find the donkeys. Where is Gameel, with those donkeys?" Shortly we found Gameel who had given the donkeys in charge of a friend and was exhilarating himself in the circle of suitors around the *ghaziyeh*.

"Now, Shehata," I said firmly, "you are trying to stage a melodrama here and I am not to be stampeded. I shall stay and visit the women's quarters and go back with Gameel, as planned."

This was too much English for the Bedouin, but my meaning was clear. "Shehata, Captain of my Caravan, go back to the tents and see that the Poet is all right. I command you. I shall return shortly with Gameel, as planned." The movie queen business worked

[181]

as usual, and he departed with much shaking of head.

Gameel being now in charge of my precious person I soon experienced regret at my adventurous spirit. Gameel, as Lieutenant of the Caravan, had been a quite faithful powerful automaton. Gameel on his own, was a very different character.

As soon as Shehata, his cousin, and only a few years older than himself, was well out of call, he changed our course, and instead of taking me to the Women's Quarters, I suddenly found myself behind them and being pulled off the path into the little ravine I had noticed earlier in the evening.

I heard in the distance the droning voice of an *Antari,* a female story-teller, as it rose above the other sounds of musical instruments. No doubt she was relating a thrilling adventure of the Bedouin hero, Antar, or of wonderful Abu Zeid.

Gameel's intent was clear. His blood had been stirred by the weird moonlight revelries of his people. Well-born in the Desert Tribe and educated at a Mission school he spoke English.

"Gameel, stop. Let go of my hand." He stopped, but did not release my hand until I added, laughing frankly in his face:

"You are very silly. You are in a dream. Wake up." Then, sternly, "Allah will punish you."

I had regained the path by now.

"Gameel, go and get the donkeys and Mohamet. I wish to return to camp."

For an instant he hesitated, then having decided something in his mind, he became the usual Gameel. The donkeys were found and we were quickly riding back

[182]

along that path towards camp without, however, Mohammet, my donkey boy.

"He is coming right along," lied Gameel. I learned
later that Mohammet never knew of our departure.

We had travelled about forty minutes in silence.
Although not desert-wise, I had a growing sense that
the direction was not right and it was quite time to be
reaching camp. Suddenly Gameel said, exultingly:

"You are alone in the Desert with me. No one will
hear you cry. You are miles away from camp. Only
I can take you there. You will be lost—die in the desert without me."

With a contraction of the solar plexus I realized the
brutal truth of this. The man was vibrant with suppressed emotion. The prospect was not alluring.

"Oh, no." I bluffed lightly. "George Washington
knows the way home."

"Rubbish!" Gameel briefly disposed of this, and with
one leap was off his saddle and had thrown the reins to
the ground. Rameses the Great, like a Western horse,
was bridle-wise and stopped. Another leap, and Gameel
had brought George Washington to a standstill. Holding
my animal's bridle firmly, the Bedouin, lithe and powerful as a panther, stood in front of me, his face on a
level with mine, not a foot apart. His eyes blazed and
his picturesque speech came fast.

"For weeks your glorious white face has filled my
heart. I cannot sleep, I cannot eat, because of you.
Night and day I am mad for you. You are mine. May
Allah forgive me. If I live, or if I die in a thousand
torments, still shall you be mine."

His face worked with emotion, the black eyes darted

[183]

lightning, the nostrils quivered like a thoroughbred animal. To match my puny muscles with his magnificent physique was futile. I had no weapon of any sort. There was no possible hope of rescue. Alone in the desert with a passion-driven animal! Something must be done, and done quickly. The adventure was becoming too colourful. He flung an iron arm around my waist to sweep me off the saddle.

"Gameel, wait," I said in a tense arresting tone. He held for an instant. His hot breath on my cheek.

"Ah, Madame, give me the honey of your lips, the sweetness of the date shall fill us. Hold not! Many white ladies come to the desert for this. That English Madame we passed yesterday. Do you not think she is kind to her dragoman? Be kind to Gameel!" This startling and wholly novel suggestion shivered me for an instant.

"Gameel, that is a lie! But no matter! I did not come into the desert for such things and you shall not spoil it for me."

Gameel did not answer, was not listening. His grip tightened. He was master of the moment and knew it. The situation was impossible. It simply could not be. It should not be. Yes, I had one weapon and I would use it. Why should I hesitate! It was a weapon I had been taught never to use upon a human being save in a matter of life and death. I felt justified in trying it now. It was a glorious opportunity. I could test it without compunction. Would it work!

"Gameel! Look at me! Look into my eyes." The words issued from my lips in a vibrant whisper. My whole soul swelled with power. *I, I* would conquer him!

Startled, the half crazy man looked in my eyes, not six inches from his. I do not know how long the silent struggle lasted. What he saw there, caused his body gradually to relax, his arms loosened their grasp, dropped to his side, his face became drained of every drop of blood, his eyes wide and staring. For an eternity were we posed thus. Then, dropping onto his knees in the sand before me, he wailed: "My God, what are you? Who are you? What have you done to me? See, the proud Gameel is on his knees before you. He will worship from afar. You are a goddess. I am your slave. I am as a reed in the wind, like water is my blood. So long as life shall last, your wish is my wish. Command me even to the ends of the earth and I will come."

I had matched my will against his—and won. I had attached my will to the great dynamic force that swings the sun, moon and stars in thier places and poured it into this puny brain to its utter confusion. "Will is the silent source of all the power of all the gods in all ages of the infinite harmony of time." It submerged, engulfed this primitive man as a chartless ship is lost in a fog. For several minutes he remained thus, pouring out broken sentences—of subjection and admiration—striking on one idea, like one coming out of a delirium.

"Now, get on your donkey and take me as quickly as possible to camp." I said it gently, for it was rather terrible to see a magnificent animal, in all the glory of its lustful strength, paralyzed into a limp and beaten thing. Trembling in every limb, he obeyed, and a half-hour's ride in silence brought us to the very welcome lights, the Poet's relieved greeting and a most acceptable bed.

I made no complaint to Shehata. This wild adventure was nobody's fault but my own and "all's well that ends well."

9. THE FAYUM HOLIDAY

The next day we pushed on, and the next. In the middle of the afternoon we had reached our immediate goal—the Fayum—and encamped a few miles in the Desert. Shehata, if allowed to dictate, never got near enough to a village to run the risk of thieving Arabs. "Low-class people," he called them, "not good."

At this point I was made aware respectfully, but firmly, that it was customary on such occasions to have a "wedding." And it was evident that I was expected to furnish the necessary for this celebration.

"What will it cost, Shehata? You know I have left all my money behind at the Shepheard Hotel."

"Would Madame like to purchase a bullock, a sheep, or a goat? The men will roast it before you and then they will dance and make merry."

"A Barbecue," quoth the Poet, "I have a gold piece."

Shehata took the English sovereign with his usual bow, but looked doubtful. He gave it to Mohamet, who, with two of the other camel boys, went off singing.

"Perhaps it will buy a goat. They will see."

In about two hours they were back empty-handed.

[186]

CARAVANING

Dejection sat upon them. But they said nothing. I called Shehata.

"The littlest goat was 40 shillings."

I was chagrined. These dusky children had not been trying to cheat us.

"Shehata, add whatever is necessary and tell them to buy a nice fat sheep and vegetables and cakes and have a real wedding for us this evening."

Smiles and whoops greeted this speech. Blithely the deputation set off for the second time to negotiate miles of desert. Others began digging a pit in the sand for the unfortunate victim which was to be sacrificed for our Fayum Holiday.

In due course the animal transported himself to the scene. Like the gorgeously attired youth of the olden days of the Incas he was decked out in coloured ribbons and a necklace of beads, another of bells. These were his Montezuma feather-robe of sacrifice. The Poet and I discreetly absented ourselves for the subsequent unpleasant details and when next we saw the animal it had assumed the usual look of cooked food and no longer suggested how near to the surface lie the cannabalistic instincts of even the most highly-civilized race of which we were pleased to think ourselves a part. Indeed we frankly enjoyed that sheep, once it was turned into human energy by the Arabs who danced before us, a highly diverting parody of what I had witnessed a few nights before in the Bedouin encampment. Gameel, the young rascal, had gotten himself up as a dancing girl. With assistance of a pillow fastened in front of him and tied in the middle around his waist he had accomplished the approved bulging frontal lines of a native charmer. "We like them fat. It is very nice and sweet, n-i-c-e," said Shehata, lingering unctuously over the last word.

Gameel's slim ankles carried silver anklets, his slim brown arms were loaded with bracelets. A native girl's headdress and basque and flowered skirt had evidently been brought back with the sheep. A white veil coquettishly covered his very masculine nose and moustache. His large black eyes rolled languorously behind kohl-covered lashes. The general effect was startlingly suggestive as he, or rather she, coquetted with her various suitors. Many a Y. M. C. A. hut was enlivened by similar actors during the Great War. According to the rules of the dance, they formed a ring around her, each seeking for her favour. Gameel did all the various acrobatic allurements, and rhythmic dances, including the *danse du ventre* of which he was past master. Louder and louder rose the rugged chant of the suitors, who accompanied their wild music with rhythmic beating of the right hand, first on the left hand, then on the knee. Clap, clap went the hands, wail, shout went the voices. Wilder and wilder danced Gameel. The excitement was at white heat when Mohamet, darting from the circle seized the rhythmically writhing form of the dance girl and carried it off into the desert while the remaining suitors set up a howl and fired a volley of revolver shots in the air.

The performance ended in a short of mirth. Mohamet had quickly dumped Gameel into a heap on the sand and then the two speedily returned and relieved their feelings by a stick fight. Every camel boy carries a heavy stick of a certain length, made of ash imported from Caramania or Nabut. Gameel, now divested of his female trappings, showed what an athlete he was by some very clever wrestling. After each victorious round he would come and bow for us. Had he forgotten a few nights before, a very different scene when he was not conqueror? If not, he gave no sign, save perhaps the deep respect of his obeisance, and an alertness to see and do a service.

"What have you done to that handsome beggar?" queried the Poet, who is no fool.

I merely smiled at her the slow, incomprehensible smile of the East.

10. THE MIRAGE

One evening strolling from camp among the tombs of Dashur I saw on our way back from the Fayum two strange-looking animals. They had sharp pointed noses and bushy tails: But they looked as big as calves. The sand was tossed into rolling dunes and they soon disappeared behind one. The night was a reddish afterglow. Shehata informed me they were Desert foxes, and that they only looked big. It was the deceiving Desert light. Hastily sneaking around the swelling dune I got another glimpse of the same two animals but now they looked no bigger than cats. It is one of the "jinks" which the Desert plays when in a whimsical mood.

For several nights, the Jackals called, a shivery sound not good to hear, and one day, suddenly before our vision in the middle of the morning's march appeared a lake with trees encircling half of it. I knew this to be a mirage and gazed at it with a stilled heart until it disappeared, as suddenly as it had come. Only one other time in all my desert experiences have I seen a mirage, and it came and went in the same unexplained way.

11. A MARKET AT EL KETTA

Starting early one morning Shehata guided the Poet and me to El Ketta where there was to be a market. All along the edge, where the fertile delta loses itself in the desert are flat fields of alfalfa or cucumbers, growing in long rows and protected from the high winds by dead stalks of the sugar cane, and groves of date palms, kept alive by the blessed nourishment of the Nile water which is carried in canals intersecting the whole tract. On different days these delta desert towns have market days when the peasants come from miles around to dispose of their live stock and farm produce, and to make purchases for the coming week.

We skirted the desert for several miles and were beginning to repent having undertaken the expedition, for the sun was scorching and the sand was disturbed by the traffic of many feet—humans, camels, donkeys, sheep, goats, cow-buffalo, even pigs, all being driven to market. Then a curious scene broken upon us and the fascination of the mob revived our jaded senses. Straggling date palms, just beginning to form fruit, gave a meagre and occasional shade. They did little to temper the heat of a windless day. A babel of raucous animal voices formed a monotonous accompaniment to the shrill hawkings of the Arab venders. There were no tents, no booths. Everything was for sale out in the open—animals, baskets, gaudy handkerchiefs, cotton goods, the ordinary black *galabeyeh*—vegetables fresh and dried. Huge baskets of oranges made brilliant piles, and there were last year's dates, strung together on sticks, or mashed into a solid block and chopped off by the pound. Children with sore eyes ran about underfoot, and the flies, the pestiferous flies, were everywhere.

Small charcoal braziers, not a foot from the sand, cooked small quantities of food while the hungry ones waited. I stopped before one of these. In a frying pan were a dozen pieces of liver sizzling in grease. An old woman stood guard and doled out this delicacy for the equivalent of three cents a piece. A customer had just finished making his purchase of two pieces which had been fished out by a forked stick and slapped into a six-inch piece of coarse brown paper, the grease dripping.

An old beldame stood near. She had some small money in her hand, enough to buy three pieces of liver. It was a serious business. She poked her skinny forefinger around in the greasy pan and transferred the selected pieces one by one to her left hand. She scorned the brown paper wrapper. But, not satisfied with her inspection, she now proceeded to return two of the fingered articles to their frying pan and select two others more to her liking. This good lady had never heard of germs, nor of such effete articles as table furniture. Wrapping two of these pieces of liver in a corner of her shawl she hobbled off to share her meal with her kind.

Two beautiful tall cone-shaped baskets now attracted my attention. I wanted them, but they were big enough for me to have gotten in them, and hidden. Shehata solved the difficulty of slinging one on each side of

A WOMAN TENDERFOOT IN EGYPT

George Washington: even then they barely missed the
ground. They swallowed his legs and his dignity all the
way back. It was a real act of devotion, and even the
Poet looked properly solemn. Pleasant it was to escape
from the noise, the heat, confusion and dirt of this typical Market Day and revel again in the comfort of our
tents in the evening-sweet desert.

12. PYRAMID DAY

The next day was Pyramid Day. That stupendous
pile has a hidden history which belongs to the Egypt of
Long Ago. The time-driven tourist who is "seeing
Egypt" while the steamer waits for her at Alexandria
has no section of her consciousness open for such impressions. She is rushed in a motor car from Cairo towards
the Pyramids along the wonderful avenue of shade
trees—whizz! bang! she has jumped out and with twenty,
fifty of her fellows, is fitted to a donkey, or a camel,
back, and started up the walled road past the Meneh
House before she has had time to get her breath. Usually her whole attention is concentrated upon the adjustment necessary to harmonize the novel sensations
provided by her mount. A voice breaks through her
mental fog, calling upon her to look at the "greatest
wonder of the ages. This Great Pyramid of Cheops built
of 2,300,000 separate blocks of yellowish limestone aver-
aging two and one-half tons; 100,000 men worked for
three months every year for twenty years; $1,750,000
was spent on radishes, onions and roots of garlic alone for
distribution among the workmen. How much for tools,

food and clothing of the workmen? It is now 450 feet high and its sides rise at an angle of 51° 50'. It covers thirteen acres of ground——" But she is not listening. She can get all this in the guide-book later, but she never does. She reluctantly lets go one hand from the saddle pommel, sweeps the wind-blown veil and hair out of her eyes and looks at the dark mass rising before her. The sun glares into her eyes. Blinded, she ducks. The camel takes a long step over a stone, and she wishes she were dead. "Is that what I have come all this way to see?" she thinks. "It is not very big—nothing to make such a fuss about. Just a lot of stones piled up. Yes! it is bigger than I thought it was." She is assisted to dismount and, once on the ground, returns to normalcy.

"Gracious, what huge blocks of stone! How can any one climb them? Look at that man being handed up by those black men in dresses! No, thanks, I'll stay on the ground. Yes, it is wonderful. Dear me, must I get on that thing again? No, I can't walk as far as the Sphinx." A deep sigh as she heroically prepares to do her duty. This time the camel's back is reached more easily, and by the time she is half-way to the Sphinx she is beginning to enjoy herself. Approaching this strange monument from the rear and almost on a level with it, she again wonders why it is not larger. Swinging round in front of it and having her photograph taken on the, by now, "darling camel" with the human-faced Lion as a background, she looks over her shoulder, and the lure of the thing that has stood there for untold generations, grips her a little. She dismounts and fills her shoes full of sand, none too clean, defiled by the hordes of tourists scattering papers, sandwiches, scraps and orange peel. She ploughs to the base of the Sphinx and looks up.

"Isn't it wonderful ?" she thinks, perhaps says. Her imagination begins to stir.

"All aboard, Party No. 35," drifts upon her and then a shrill voice, "Hurry up, Mrs. Smith, you'll be late!" Back to the camel, to the Meneh House, to the motor car, to the Kasrel-Nil Bridge, to the Cairo Hotel. A trip through the bazaars, cigarettes and perfume of the Orient are hers, a mosque or two are visited: then back to Alexandria and to the Steamer. She has seen Egypt!

I well remember my two personal encounters with the Great Wonder of Cheops. I have made its acquaintance "from the ground up" and "inside and out." Much has been done to stop the rascality of the guides, but there are still some unscrupulous ones and the stories are not infrequent of a woman or even a man being held up in some dark passage of the interior and terrorized into giving ransom for safe exit. The day before I ventured in, a gentleman thus victimized handed over his heavy pocket-book so meekly that the bandit was deceived. He brought the gullible American to the surface quickly and, once out, that gentleman whipped out a revolver, demanded his pocketbook and marched the culprit to the Police Station. Usually these "hold ups" mean a bribe of a few shillings or of a gold piece and, while not dangerous to life, are very wearing on the nerves.

Shehata protected me from all this of course. He got the Policeman stationed near the entrance to shoo off the hordes of persistent, licensed guides, he having previously engaged one of them—"a friend of mine who is nice and honest." Shehata always had a tried and trusted friend for every emergency. Alone with my two guides I started down the steep incline from the entrance. The Poet, being never very much inclined to the strenuous life, sat on the outside and counted the minutes. Indeed it is no place for babes and weaklings. The physical difficulties are about equal to glacier climbing. Not many women have their ambition to ruin their shoes and stockings and dignity. I slid and jumped, was dragged and lowered and lifted over rough stone passages and tiny chambers. I negotiated a well twenty feet down and three feet wide with only iron footholds, and pitch black, save for the candles we carried. The air was close and heavy. A strange experience truly. One lost all count of modern life. My two long-robed, turbaned escorts only helped the picture. Further and further back into the past I wandered, when suddenly like the hubbub of a wild west show, came the cat-calls and yodels of a party of Italian youths. They might have been French, American or English. They were at the noisy age. They made the silent, dead and empty thing hideous with their shouts and shuffles. Sweeping like a cyclone through the rockbound passages, shrieking and pounding up and down the steep incline of the hall of illumination; waking the echoes of forgotten lives in the chamber of the King, poking sticks in the ventilating shafts, jumping in and out of the sarcophagus where majesty had lain while forests were being made and new river beds were being cut through living rock. They finally passed out leaving a shattered silence.

The faces of my two guides, wore the inscrutable Oriental look. My visions were gone, we climbed the last

incline and I was restored to a thankful Poet, who had
been standing sentinel, walking back and forth, in fear
that my long absence meant disaster.

"See," quoth she, "a fish to the water, a goat to the
rocks," and handed me the following:

NEAR THE PYRAMIDS

Not crowned am I, nor yet am I cast out,
Filt'ring through interstices of being
Are the Sun-shafts, the golden glints seeing
My soul point towards a diadem, no doubt
Assails the Ultimate, but all about
Me falters from the Outward, agreeing
With long tests of days, human decreeing
Falsifies my inner best, no faint shout
Of consummation joys my yearning heart,
Great Gizeh's Height directs, with fixed strength
My soul, withal my weakening, and the
Tortured, devious within to start
Initiations, all along the length
Of Ways laid out, I, stumbling, walk
    toward Thee.

Then came the ever-fascinating ride back to our desert
home. How sweet it seeemed and superbly peaceful, not
the quietude of a vacant mind, but the purposeful peace
of static harmony.

It was some three weeks later that I was able to make
the ascend of the Great Pyramid. After a "trip up the
Nile," we were again caravaning in the desert, and the
time was growing short when the marvellous holiday

must end. A dose of enteric fever, developed from carelessness in eating a green salad at Assouan, had laid me low. A week of misery, punctuated by the excitement of an English doctor dashing over the desert on a glorious Arabian steed which he pulled from a full gallop to a standstill right at the open door of my tent, and softened by the devotion of my friend, the Poet, and of the devoted Shehata, and the last day of our stay had arrived with the Great Pyramid as yet unclimbed by me.

The Poet had always firmly refused to even consider such a feat. Indeed I found that very few women ever attempted the climb. Principally the English, now and then an American, never a French woman. It was clearly a freak interest.

However for me, the ascent had to be made; so, very "groggy on the pins" as Shehata put it, using one of his quaint Englishisms, I arrived at the foot of the Pyramid that towered above me interminably.

Two guides were obligatory. With the faithful Shehata on one side, and the "friend of mine," who had assisted when doing the interior, on the other side and the third able-bodied Arab scrambling ahead and giving a well-directed yank when my person did not heave up in good form, we started to climb the granite blocks, one by one. Owing to the facing of stone having long since disappeared, they are like gigantic steps. The northwest angle has the greater number of ledges and about half way up, there is a recess, perhaps six feet in depth. With the shame of a traveller, I must now confess that at this point a vertigo seized me and I was a prey to the most abject fear. A wild desire to pitch myself off into space possessed me and an equally wild fear that I would do so, made me a battleground of nerves and will.

It was like the worst kind of nightmare, a death grip of horror, a dethronement of will and reason. Had some lost soul, some demon, been able to slip into a body weakened by illness, I could not have agonized more. Like the young miss in the song, I "could not get up, I could not get down."

It was an awful five minutes. Ostensibly I was recovering breath from the climb. In reality the terrors of the damned were upon me. The impassive faces of my three dusky attendants, all sprung from a race which despises women, gave me no help. As a *white* woman I was in a class by myself in their minds, but I would have to continue to remain superwoman, or shatter their traditions.

By a supreme effort of will I announced that we would continue the ascent. I fully expected to be dashed to the bottom a broken bundle, but in time the broad resting-place of the apex was accomplished. Trying to forget the terror of the descent which hung like a pall over my senses, I looked upon the broad delta of the Nile,—then fertile with alfalfa,—on the distant palms of Memphis, the shadowy shapes of the lesser Sakkara pyramids, on the tragic Sphinx. All was touched with the glow of a setting sun—a scene of mysterious beauty, the lure of a million years. One indeed looked from a great height; one saw as the eagle sees. One stood on the very top of Egypt and watched it floating away in waves of memory that lapped the shore of eternity itself.

The miracle of an Egyptian sunset was born before my eyes as one by one the pyramid groups at Gizeh rose out of the afterglow and the Sphinx at last was vested with a mystery which in the hot glare of noon is lacking. Now could I rearrange these noble piles of masonry as the original architects had planned them, proud and mighty with their temples and the long approaches leading to each one of them from the East.

Suddenly the obsession of fear flew away also. Fear had no place in that time-tried scene. I started down. I slid and slipped and was lifted from little precipice to precipice, realizing again how powerful and wiry were these sons of the desert; for they scrambled about like cats, apparently quite unimpeded by the long robes they wore; while I, clad in a short skirt and assisted by three of them, puffed and panted and at times inwardly quaked —but, though lacking muscle, I had the *dinars* they coveted, and, in due time, was brought down in safety to the anxious Poet, and parted from the much-prized English-Egyptian pounds, the *summum bonum* of most Arabs, high or low.

However this time I found that the Poet, though expressing concern, had been enjoying herself immensely and had been "doing" the Pyramid in her way with apparently much more soul satisfaction than I.

PAEON

I strayed along the maze, was lost awhile,
As one in forest stumbles neath the shades
To play with Will o'wisp which so evades
The idle chase: and then with simple smile
I rested, claiming Nature to beguile
My restless soul; and now the glorious glades
Of sun-swept pathway open and then fades
All lethargy, I am awake, the Nile,

[199]

A WOMAN TENDERFOOT IN EGYPT

And Egypt's Soulful Sands have taught me well
To know I may not doze again, nor play,
But waking, live, there's love and life to tell,
There's destiny to learn, and what I may
Obtain I give the gods for asphodel,
As offering for freedom won To-day.

It was dreary business going back to civilization, but
we of the West must carry on the torch, and one morning
our much-labelled luggage was trundled on board the boat
train. Shehata, officiating for the last time, was very sad,
but his grief did not prevent his gently reminding us that,
if he had served us well, would we recommend him to our
friends? He presented a beautiful bouquet of flowers,
which arrived by a cousin—masses of fragrant tuberoses,
heavily-scented pink stocks, and roses fresh and dewy.
He bent over my hand with the grace of a courtier and
kissed it and then paid like homage to the Poet. Then he
made the native salaam, touching his fingers to his lips,
his cheeks and forehead. With his hand on his heart he
watched us fade out of sight. The train slipped gently
on the rails towards Alexandria. The Desert Days for
that year were over.

BOOK III

EGYPT OF LONG AGO

MEMORIES OLD AND NEW

From out illimitless Time echoes come
Of sometimes when we were together, dear,
  .   .   .   .   .   .

And in my spirit life I gain thee now
It is as though a tortured veil were rent
And through the widening rift an immense
Futurity extends. Sweet Soul, out of Time,
                 Who art Thou?
                     CELIA LOUISE CRITTENDEN

CHAPTER XIX

THE HOUSE OF LIGHT

THE INITIATION OF KING SETHRON: AN EXPLORATION INTO THE FOURTH DIMENSION

*"Instinctively he read the giant Page before him . . .
His mind became a mirror wherein the attributes of
. . . things are reflected and enter his field of consciousness . . . For man himself is but a thought pervading the
ocean of mind."*

ALGERNON BLACKWOOD in "The Centaur."

I DO not know what persons usually find when they travel in Egypt. Pretty much, I fancy, what they are looking for,—as elsewhere. I was seeking the past, to reconstruct the life that had blossomed, fruited and died, so very long ago. "Seek and ye shall find," said the great Occult Teacher of Jerusalem. And in seeking to know the past of the Great Pyramid, I found a strange something that I shall describe, rather than explain.

This is a story of the religion of the Ancient Egyptians, and especially of the worship of Ammon-Ra and of Osiris. These Great Gods of the Living and the Dead flourished mightily when the priesthood was at the highest power. Much occult knowledge had been brought over from the Atlantean time and transmitted secretly from century to century, through the priesthood.

[203]

A WOMAN TENDERFOOT IN EGYPT

THE SOLAR EYE IMPERSONATED

In the rise and fall of the Dynasties and of Empires, the power of the priest fluctuated also, but there was never a time when the sacred and secret knowledge was not passed on, generation after generation. Sometimes it was even given out in part to the people, and much was known by the majority of the priests; at others the High Priests, only, had the knowledge, which meant power, and with a clear vision of mass-psychology, circulated strange myths and superstitions which bound the people slavishly to their religion, and kept filled the coffers of the Lord High Rulers of the Temples. These understood many of the laws governing consciousness—the power of the will and of "suggestion." They practised the theory of vibration, and of levitation, and could work some of the lesser miracles, which depended upon the co-operation of the elementals. A few prophets among them lived the pure and exalted life necessary to seership; but the majority wore their religion as a cloak for self-gratification, and the pleasures of the body were paramount.

Perhaps it is not generally known that the second and the first Great Pyramids were connected underground with the Temple of the Sphinx and for several hundred years were used for certain stages of the spiritual development of the Initiates into the priesthood.

[204]

THE HOUSE OF LIGHT

My leap from the present to past, happened several years ago, during my first visit to Egypt on the night that I heard "Aïda" in the Desert, which I shall now describe as it may have had something to do with my strange experience. That is a knot for the psychoanalyst to unravel.

When we arrived in Cairo the air was full of the wonderful gala performance that was to be given at the Great Pyramid to honour a visiting potentate, an Eastern prince who was a guest of the British authorities.

At the time, I was not interested in the historical side of the pageant, but the idea of "Aïda" on the banks of the Nile in its own setting—the real luscious Egyptian moonlight with the real Pyramid of Gizeh forming a background—did capture my imagination, and I therewith parted from much gold and took away instead two pieces of paper, *billets de placement,* which represented seats in a front box.

An invitation had come for an over-night visit to a friend's caravan which had been brought within five miles of the Great Pyramid. The Poet, my companion on this occasion also, and I, were on tiptoe over this opportunity to get our first glimpse of desert life and rode out in the golden afternoon to this very luxurious camp which made a few dots on the endless expanse of tawny sand. After a leisurely dinner, beautifully cooked by another pot-black treasure, we watched the brilliant sky draw down around, warm and intimate. The stars seemed so close we could almost reach up and pluck them from the deep blue canopy of night. A faint, tangy, desert-wind tempered the warmth. An attentive dragoman placed rugs

[205]

over us as we lay in steamer-chairs enjoying the after-meal coffee, and well-being.

The performance was to begin at ten o'clock, when the full moon would be riding the heavens.

"Swiftly walk over the Western Wave, Spirit of Night,
When all through the long and lone daylight
Thou weavest dreams of joy and fear
Which make thee so terrible and dear, swift be thy flight."

These scraps of Shelley's inspiration were sweetly drifting through my mind, when we were interrupted by the appearance of Beauty, a riding dromedary, and her boy, Mohamet. Beauty was attired in her very best trappings, sniffing and parting her lips, softly, now and then, at having to work overtime, and do a "night-stunt" after the usual day's work. The Poet as usual, had selected a dromedary for her transportation. At the command of her "boy," she kneeled obediently, and the Poet, by means of a chair ascended to the comfortable seat of Oriental rugs arranged between Beauty's humps.

Once up, and started upon Beauty, the Poet began a series of complicated but monotonous motions corresponding to the long and peculiar gait of the dromedary. She described them as "a long pull out, a wiggle, another wiggle, and a jerk back, a long pull out, etc." It required a well-working spine and a sea-sick-proof stomach, to enjoy Beauty, and I, also as usual, was content with the less princely, but more comfortable, donkey. Bidding our hosts a temporary farewell, for on this occasion they were in the foolish-virgin class, and had neglected to secure tickets for this most popular event, we started forth in charge of a guide.

There was a certain excitement in the Eastern sky which told us that Diana had summoned her hunting dogs and was preparing to fare forth, and that the Lady Moon in all her fullest glory was about to grace the heavens and to give, to the already entrancing night, a greater witchery. Three-quarters of an hour brought us to a scene, the grandeur, charm and mystery of which it seems impossible to portray. It remains stamped upon my memory like an Arabian Night's Dream.

In front of the Great Pyramid of Gizeh, between it and the Meneh House, had been built a stage of heroic proportions, surrounded by palms and flowering trees; then an orchestra pit, and boxes and seats to accommodate 2,000 persons. These were packed, to overflowing, with an audience that came out from Cairo.

It was with difficulty we forced our way through the crowd, roped beyond, and squeezed into two rickety chairs as the performance began.

What a picture! Directly above the apex of the Great Pyramid, which loomed to almost interminable heights in front of us, rode the full moon in a brilliant, scintillating, sensuous, blue-arching curtain. On the Pyramid itself were ranged rows of Egyptian soldiers in their picturesque costumes and at the base behind the platform-stage, were hundreds of mounted Bedouins, their magnificent horses with gorgeous trappings and their dark handsome faces set in the burnoose and flowing billowy robes of white. Then came the scarlet-touched uniforms of some mounted guards with lances, then the stage—then the orchestra, and, rising tier after tier, the audience.

A WOMAN TENDERFOOT IN EGYPT

The *elite* of resident and visiting Egypt was there, including several royal princes, brilliant in scarlet and gold lace.
All was lit by the moon's effulgence, with no counterfeit
light whatever.

The Nile scene of "Aïda" was marvellously done by the
caste of French and Italian singers, which included some
famous names. But the details of nomenclature did not
register. It was the eternal beauty of the place, accen-
tuated and focused by humans, that mattered, a blending
of the finite with the infinite. On these sands where
man's work had endured for ages, while generations of
men had come and gone and would come and go, beauty
would unroll itself by day, by year, by century and the
race of men would be born, flower and die, and be born
again—even as the seasons. There is no death in the
universal. The drop slips into the shining sea, the shining sea continues forever and ever, *but*, the drop is no
more. As humanity, man continues forever and a day,
perhaps, but what of the individual, of the drop?
"How careless of the single life!" No wonder, in those
luscious, mysterious nights, a religion should flourish
which accepts the merging of the finite into the infinite!

We went back to our princely tents in the desert guided
by the pervasive moon that now at 1 A. M. was looking
a little wan.

Tucked into a real spring bed, mattress and all, I
looked at the rich Oriental rug spread on the sand and
on the heavily-embroidered inner wall of our canvas
room, this pin-point of luxury in all the vastness of arid-
ity about. I drifted off to the borders of the real from
the unreal and wondered the same old wonder: What

is the shadow, what the substance? Who is the master and who the slave?

This imagination that we play with, is it not the infinite? Are we not strung upon it as jewels upon a chain, the best we can ever hope for to perfect the jewel? In so doing, can we contribute to ultimate Beauty? The questions lost themselves in the cobwebs of sleep.

Then suddenly I was startled into wide wakefulness by the yelp of a jackal. Throwing a cloak about me, I went to the door of the tent and looked upon the Eastern sky where dawn was just breaking. I felt an irresistible desire to kneel and prostrate myself before the rising sun-god, Ammon-Ra. Down in the sand, prone on my face I dropped, and with a strange wonder in my heart found myself performing some strange rite of worship and repeating strange words of an unknown formula. I certainly was not asleep, for I was up and moving—but the tent and the Poet had gone out of my consciousness, and I was again in the Fire Chamber of the Great Pyramid, the interior of which I had visited the morning before as a preliminary to the evening's performance.

Now it seemed to me, that I again stood in that little room of stone walls and a rough altar, and that I caught the vision of its purpose which I am about to describe, and which solved for me the riddle of what had transpired in long-forgotten days in that mysterious pile of masonry, and suggested the reason for its strange passages and channels, at different angles and on different levels,

After my obeisance to the rising sun-god, I still kneeled on the sand. The scene faded and I beheld a man clad in kingly garments. He was coming from the

[209]

Temple of the Sphinx by an underground passage which communicated first with the Pyramid of Kephren and then through the Temple grounds by an avenue of sacred tamarisks to the entrance of the Great Pyramid. This incredible structure seemed to him already ages old. In it was the mummy of Cheops truly, but the man striding towards it, knew that it had also been built

AMMON-RA
The God of the Living and of the Dead

for the Initiation Ceremonies of the Priests of the great Ammon-Ra: that in the days of Egypt's splendour, the Kings must also be initiates of the god, and Cheops was initiated in his own Pyramid long before the outside of it was finished, and when he was laid to rest it was not in the King's Chamber, but between that and the Hall of Illumination where the little chambers rise tier on tier. Above the four-foot passage of solid rock, his sarcophagus was placed, and in it, at last, his mummy. A cunning device truly, which served for several thousand years to leave his mortal remains undisturbed. They were still intact at this time in which I seemed to be, which was in the XXIII Dynasty, when Sethron, with whom I felt identified, sticking like a fly to the polished surface of the northern face of the Pyramid, climbed to the entrance, some eighty feet up, from a garden of palms and oleanders below.

There he found the entrance guarded by two figures in long white robes. They silently challenged him. He brushed them aside with dignity.

"I, brethren, Sethron, the King, though but the humblest priest among you, have been summoned to the Fiery Ordeal and, if worthy, to the Chamber of the King," he said.

The time had come for the King of Memphis to assume the leopard skin of the priest, and several tests must he pass before he could lay himself down in the Chamber of the King and, his body guarded by four Angels, one for the north, others for the east, and south, and west, release his soul to wander into the Territory of the Dead and to seek knowledge of the life beyond, while yet living the life of earth.

If he failed to pass the tests he could not remain King, for Hotep the High Priest, was all-powerful, and would soon find means to replace so unworthy a representative of Heaven and Earth.

A WOMAN TENDERFOOT IN EGYPT

It was the supreme test of his ambition and of his life, for destruction of his body lurked in every test. To fail at any point meant—death.

Once inside, the would-be Initiate passed down a steep tunnel of rock, so narrow that his elbows, if extended, would have touched the walls; so low in places that he was obliged to crawl on hands and knees for a few feet, and dark, absolutely black, unless the King himself had the power to create the astral light to show him the way.

Suddenly Sethron found himself on the brink of a chasm. His inner sense gave warning just in time and also told him that the passage continued on the other side of this chasm, which seemed to yawn to unfathomed depths below. How to get across, was the ordeal—he paused, waiting for his inner guide to speak. Then a faint voice seemed to say, "Take two paces to the right, raise your right arm and pull the cord." This done Sethron's upward extended hand felt a knotted rope. This he pulled. There was a rush and a rumble and something slid into place at his feet. Cautiously examining this, it proved to be a heavy plank a foot wide, extending over the chasm into the unknown blackness. Without hesitation he footed his way along this narrow support—the slightest tremor or misstep would have dashed him into the black depths—and in a few paces, arrived across the chasm. The silent voice now instructed, "Take two paces to the left, reach up your left hand and pull." He obeyed, and his extended left hand encountered a knotted rope, which he pulled as before; there was a rumble and a rush under him and the bridge disappeared. The Chasm of Fear had been safely passed.

THE HOUSE OF LIGHT

Sethron had proceeded along a completely dark passage for some distance when he encountered a wall of solid rock. No opening of any kind was discoverable. It was the Gate of Despair and Discouragement. For a long time he waited, commanding the impenetrable rock to depart. His will to open the barrier before him gathered in strength until he seemed to be emitting sparks of concentrated energy while his body grew in power. Then suddenly he heard the silent voice again.

"It is well, you have conquered the force of darkness. Stand in the center, extend your arms like a cross, press your body against the wall and with all your force push towards the right side." Sethron did as he was commanded, the whole of the obstructive wall, including the place upon which he was standing, turned a complete half circle and the King found himself on the other side of the Gate of Despair.

At the end of a very long tunnel which broke upon his vision was a lurid glow and he knew that the Trial by Fire was about to begin.

He proceeded quickly to the end of this narrow rock passage where he found himself in a chamber filled with leaping flames. At his feet the flames were not more than a foot high, so that he could see opposite a wall of dancing, curling, crackling spirals of orange and red flashes, arising, apparently, from the rough stone floor, in a mad dance to the rock ceiling into which they melted. The King knew that he must pass this fiery curtain. How far it extended he knew not. Advancing to the centre about ten feet over the sharp points of the floor, partly rock and partly breaking into low flames, he turned and faced the fiery wall. Without fear he addressed the gods of the Underworld:

"O Anubis, the Dog-faced! who keeps ever faithful guard; O Horus, the Hawk-headed! who watches over the souls of men, hear my prayer, lead me to pass the portal, and receive my worship."

HORUS

As he spoke a pathway through the fire appeared before him, and as he advanced boldly over the still flaming floor, he beheld an altar with a figure of Anubis seated on his throne on the left side and a figure of Horus seated on his throne on the right side. They were terrible, colossal—indifferent. Upon the altar

[215]

stood two large chalices, one of shining black as though fashioned from a colossal black diamond; the other glowing red, as though it were cut out of a ruby. Both were semi-transparent, showing within their bowls, a glowing liquid which bubbled red in the black chalice, orange in the red chalice. Grasping the ruby cup in his right hand and the diamond cup in his left hand, King Sethron extended his arms towards the two gods, and thus addressed them:

"O Mighty Ones, who rule the fate of Man! unto You I offer the libations of all my good acts and of all my evil acts. Grant me a safe passage through the Kingdom, O Anubis! Guard me to the Kingdom of Immortal Souls, O Horus!" Thereupon he threw the libation of the ruby cup upon the feet of the god Horus and the libation of the diamond cup upon the feet of Anubis, bowed thrice and turned to go. The wall of living flames again separated for him, the flinty points hurt not his naked feet, the flames closed behind him. The terrible Trial by Fire had been passed.

But where now? To the right was an opening along a rocky passage, similar to the one through which he entered the Fire Chamber, and which he could discern at an equal distance on his left. Which way was he to go? No voice came to his aid. The flames danced and crackled behind him. They seemed advancing. He must choose, and choose quickly.

It would seem as though he should turn to the right to go onward with his journey and yet—something warned.

"O Ammon-Ra, Maker of Light," he cried, "it is Thee I seek. Guide my footsteps," and, as he spake, the Inner Voice replied:

THE HOUSE OF LIGHT

"To the right thou mayest go on—Yes,—but to the Underworld never to return. Retrace thy footsteps, until thou comest to the gate that leadeth to the Hall of Illumination."

To the left the Initiate turned again into the blackness, thereby escaping the fate of some who are not wise enough, and who, turning to the right, soon meet the solid rock from which there is no escape, and perish miserably there.

A faint halo of light now hovered around the head of the Initiate, the reward of the ordeals already passed successfully, and this enabled him to proceed with more ease and to halt before the outline of an archway cut in the rock, on his right hand, which he could never have noticed in the darkness through which he had passed before. To open the gate he must find the password, or the means to conquer this barrier to his full illumination. As he stood before it, wrestling with his soul, he heard faint strange sweeps of sounds. It was not music, as he understood it, but a rhythmic rush of deep notes that seemed to come from afar, beginning as a small spiral and increasing in volume and size, until finally they reached the spot where he stood and swirled around him, from left to right, in a great *booming* which, nevertheless, seemed to make no real sound. It was his own Will, objectivized to his consciousness. Sethron was caught in it as in the vortex of a maelstrom, which carried him along irresistibly through the barrier, which crumbled to naught before the on-sweeping spirals—along a passage that suddenly widened into a great hall of most peculiar construction. Sethron stood in a maze at the foot of a long, steep incline not more than five feet wide from which, rising, tier on tier, and ever receding into the distance, were rows of granite shelves or ledges, all following the same sharp incline upwards. Upon wider, lower levels, reclined a large company of the Initiates of the Great Ammon-Ra, assembled to receive the newcomer. They were clothed in white and about each glowed the nimbus of illumination. This spiritual light was a radiant, luminous blue, spreading around the Initiate in greater, or lesser, volume, according to his spiritual power. In it vibrated the colour bands which formed the aura of each priest, exquisite orange next the body, then a crimson, green, blue and yellow. Some of the auras of the high Initiates vibrated the higher violet and ruby. The effect to Sethron's startled vision, now opened to the spiritual colours, was that of a hundred ovals of light, shot through with jewel-like bands of colour, which glowed with a brilliancy that is not found on land or sea.

The King's advent was greeted by no sound nor move, on the part of this exalted company. One more test must be safely passed, another of Nature's laws conquered, before Sethron could attain to the King's Chamber at the far top of this Hall of Illumination.

It was the Law of Specific Gravity. By no other way than by employing levitation, could Sethron travel up the steep and slippery incline to the goal of his desires and to an ultimate place among the Initiates of Ammon-Ra. Even as Christ many years later walked upon the water, so Sethron, the King of Memphis, walked up that steep ascent. By an act of will, not dynamic this time but quiet as a summer sea at sunset, he changed the polarity of his physical atoms and his body, losing half its weight, floated up to higher level, and Sethron passed into the Chamber of the King. There, his body guarded by the four angels, he took a strange journey into many worlds where we cannot follow him. Later he emerged successfully and rejoined the luminous company in the Hall of Illumination. They now arose and greeted him as brother, with simple ceremony. The leopard skin of priesthood was draped upon him, the High Priest Hotep prostrated his body four times before him as King, and the Osiris Sceptre of Power was placed in his right hand, the Ankh or Key of Life in his left——

I heard the cry of a jackal, shivering in from the outside.

The Poet and the tent and I in it, came back, as a curtain rolls up on another scene. Was it the same cry that I had left when I went excursioning into the fourth dimension? I shall never know, for the Poet was asleep.

CHAPTER XX

ACROSS THE BRIDGE OF TIME

THE PRIESTESS OF EDFU TEMPLE

"For of old the Sun, our sire,
  Came wooing the mother of men,
  Earth, that was virginal then,
Vestal fire to his fire.
Silent her bosom and coy,
  But the strong god sued and press'd:
And born of their starry nuptial joy
  Are all that drink of her breast."

WILLIAM WATSON, "Ode in May."

THE Poet, being a Poet, received the account of my friend, King Sethron, and his strange doings in the House of Light, if not with entire credence at least with an open mind, that it had "really happened," and was not just a "pipe dream" of a busy imagination.

I might almost have begun to wonder about it myself, if another experience had not clapped down on the head of circumstances and made me ask with Algernon Blackwood, what is the present, what is the past? Since nothing is lost, why should we not, on occasion, turn back history's page and read a fragment from the Akasic Records?

ACROSS THE BRIDGE OF TIME

A few days after the Desert Visit and Great Pyramid excitement, the Poet and I, being true devotees of Nin—that fat-faced god who presides over the destinies of Travellers in the Desert—found ourselves revelling in the charms of Luxor, and then, again on the steamer for the Second Cataract. We were "doing Egypt" that year as any self-respecting tourist should do it.

On the left bank of the Nile and not far above Luxor, which was the ancient Thebes, nestles the town of Edfu and, a mile or so inland, the most beautiful of all the Temples. Its present-day state of preservation enables one to reconstruct its past glories; and in it is embodied the purest form of Egyptian architecture. It is said that the original temple was built in the Third Dynasty, about 2100 B. C., by Imhotep, the Grand Vizier of Zoser, a man of great learning and power who also devised a means of transporting and lifting the huge stones of which the Pyramids are constructed—which has always intrigued architects of subsequent ages. This ancient temple passed into decay and hardly a stone of its foundation remained when, in the reign of Ptolemy III., the Priests of Ammon-Ra rebuilt it as it was from the original plans of Imhotep, which had been secretly cherished by the priests and safely hidden for some 1,800 years. The hiding place was revealed to a priest in a dream, or vision, in which the great master, Imhotep, appeared to the priestly student of occultism, and instructed him to rebuild the temple to the God Ammon-Ra. This great work was completed in 57 B. C. Robert Hichens in his book on Egypt devotes a whole chapter to the wonders and beauties of this Temple of the Inward Flame, of the Secret Soul, dedicated to Horus the Hawk-headed—Son

[221]

of Isis and Osiris—the Apollo of the old Egyptian World,
crowned with many crowns—the youth who fought
Set, the murderer of his Father. The Temple was also
dedicated to Ammon or Anum—God of the Dead—and
Ra—Sun—that is, Ammon-Ra, the God of the Living and
of the Dead.

"Its beauty of form," says Hichens, "is like Music.
Edfu is supreme, any change in it could only be harm-
ful—pure and perfect a design—broad propylon, great
open courtyard—next pillared galleries, halls, chambers,
sanctuary, from colonnade and hypostyle hall, thus slowly
to the Sanctuary, the meaning of it all—the sacred
heart of the building. In no other temple does one
have the same consciousness of the sacred shrine heart
of it, the house Divine of the Hidden One."

But all this was later knowledge. At the moment
which I am about to describe, I knew nothing of the
Temple, not even its name. Absorbed in the wonders
of ancient Thebes, I had taken no thought for the sights
of the morrow.

In the sunset, seated outside my cabin door on the
deck of the little Nile steamer after leaving Luxor, I was
watching the mysterious Egyptian landscape glide by.
It was the distinctive silhouette of date palms with
here and there a minaret or a square tower focusing
the outline, the whole black against a crimson and purple sky. The tropical sun was painting the great sweep
of the sky in regal flame rays and the twilight hush held
one in the grip of other things. The consciousness of
one's strenuous, bursting, avid, Occidental life receded,
and, into the glowing silence of the departing sun, I
slipped into the doings of the past. Though conscious

[222]

that I was seated upon a camp stool on the deck of a Nile steamer and that my eyes were open, for over twenty minutes I heard and saw the following drama enacted before me.

THE VISION OF THE PRIESTESS AT EDFU TEMPLE

It was sunset. The evening glow still lingered in the outer court of the Temple where two rows of white-robed priests had assembled to greet a half-dozen Novitiates—young girls dressed in white, with long flowing veils over their faces and girdles of gold. Their bare legs and sandal-covered feet (the straps crossing straight over the instep) kept time in a slow graceful dance to the music of instruments, small harps with few strings, and cymbals. The graceful figures carried garlands of leaves and flowers, the bare arms waved rhythmically. Attendants in long striped robes, bound by brilliant sashes, held lighted torches. Behind the rows of priests a few men and women were standing in groups. Two beautifully-wrought urns on high tripods of bronze gave forth incense vapours. A group of High Priests stood near the Northern incense urn.

Only the six dancing maidens, the Novitiates, were allowed in the paved inner space. Outside the Temple doors was a multitude of men, women and children, talking, murmuring, gesticulating. They seemed to have just escorted the maidens to the Temple and were waiting for the parents to be done with the final rites of relinquishing their daughters to the service of the Great God Ammon-Ra and his son Horus, the Hawk-headed, to whom the Temple was dedicated.

A WOMAN TENDERFOOT IN EGYPT

Outwardly there was rejoicing, inwardly the hearts of at least one father and mother were dripping blood— tears of anguish. The maidens were supposed to be willing Novitiates, but Meral two days before had been a happy, care-free child of fifteen, when the startled parents received papyri setting forth the Great Honour above all price which had been conferred upon their daughter, whom the god had "summoned to his service."

There was no escape, the priests were all-powerful among the people, and even among the upper class, to which Meral belonged, there was small hope of getting the Roman local ruler to withstand the Priesthood; and alas, the First High Priest, no other than the Great Rahotep himself, had by some evil chance come to know of the charms of Meral. Now there was nothing to do but say good-bye. She was for ever lost to them.

It was the feast of the High Noon. Always maidens were accepted at this time and the groups of High Priests stood appraising the young womanhood which was to enter the life of the temple and the service of the Most High.

Rahotep's piercing glance, his eyes like black diamonds, scrutinized each swaying figure as the measures of the dance proceeded, until he found the figure he sought. No need to see the face, he knew its flower beauty. More than a week before when Meral had sought the Temple and, while praying at one of the smaller altars, her veil had slipped exposing her face and throat. No one was near, no one but the granite figure of Horus, to whom she prayed. As she glanced up, she was startled at the eyes of the God; they seemed alive, and to move, then they became deep holes of nothingness again. No,

[224]

Rahotep looked not for the veiled face of Meral now, but for a slender upheld arm which bore a bracelet of turquoise and beaten gold, the gift of Ammon-Ra which accompanied the papyrus roll of dread summons to the Temple service.

Into the High Priest's eyes darted a fiery gleam. "Tomorrow," he thought, "she shall be the Bride of the Sun. Ammon-Ra shall take her at High Noon."

The dance over, the maidens rushed to their parents for a last embrace, and then in formal procession, surrounded by rows of priests chanting, of musicians and of torch-bearers, the Novitiates passed between the two great central columns into the great Outer Hall of the Temple. Its walls were marvellously carved, wonderful tapestries covered the lower stone squares. Here at the upper end were the High Priestess and a group of Novitiates and Priestesses awaiting the newcomers. The six maidens joined this group and the procession passed into the Inner Great Hall.

Rahotep and two High Priests disappeared into the Holy of Holies, the Inner Sanctuary, where none but the very highest were allowed to enter.

That night the moon was riding her silver boat low in the heavens, and Meral stood long on the roof of the chamber in the women's quarter of the Temple, which she shared with the six new Novitiates. Her heart was bitter with loneliness for her home and her parents and dread for the future. But she was young and the witchery of the night spoke to her of Basadi, the young priest whom she had met by chance at the Taran Well, that lonely well on the outskirts of the village. One day, thinking herself alone, her veil had slipped; and the tall, handsome youth in white silk and priestly girdle had stopped his rapid stride transfixed by the vision of beauty. His eyes told her; and something stayed her hand for a second as she modestly reached for the veil to readjust it. It was steel and magnet, flower and sun, youth and love. Meral met him several times at the Taran Well, and Basadi had told her that the fair lotus of herself was worth more to him than a career, and that as soon as his novitiate's vows were fulfilled, he would renounce the priesthood, which was the open road to power and gratified ambition, and, since his father's house would be closed to him, he would take up a humble trade, even though it was no more than a water carrier, so that he might possess the fair Meral, and know the heaven of her smile. Yes, she thought, surely at least she would be under the same roof as Basadi, the thrilling, wonderful youth.

A Priestess broke in upon her thoughts.

"Thou must now seek thy couch, my child, for to-morrow's Sun will bring thee great joy. Thou hast been selected from all others for the Great Honour of becoming the 'Bride of the Sun.' The Great Rahotep hath said it. Sleep well that thy beauty may be worthy to offer to our Glorious Most High, the Ammon-Ra."

Bride of the Sun, what did that mean, a holy union with the God of the Temple! How unworthy she was! How could so excellent a thing happen to her, little Meral, who loved Basadi. Loved him it is true, but not so much as a chaste kiss had ever passed between them. Meral rejoiced that she could approach the Glorious One with a pure heart. She would dedicate her life to the exalted and the Most High. She dreamed

[226]

her gentle dreams, not knowing how else to prepare.

At eleven o'clock the next morning, a procession was formed of all the Priestesses and the Acolytes and the Novitiates, which proceeded from the Northern side of the Temple to the Great Central Hall. Here it joined a procession of Priests, coming from the Southern side. Incense burned. The eyes of the colossal stone gods glowed, music of harps and voices rose in a solemn chant. Torches cast picturesque lights into the partial gloom, which always prevailed in this vast Hall. The only daylight came filtering through the huge carved columns of the outer Hall, the square centre of whose roof was opened to the sun. All were robed in long flowing garments of soft white, gold-embroidered.

Meral was in a daze of fear and awe, anticipating, she knew not what. She saw that at last a priest left the long double column of his brothers, who were disappearing with measured tread through an open archway on the South side of the Hall. He stood beside her, motioning to her to remain. The Priestesses were disappearing through an archway on the Northern side. The great Rahotep had passed quite close to her, and entered the Holy of Holies. She dropped on her knees in worship before a statue of the god.

The priest beside her waited a moment for her prayer, then taking her hand said, "Come, Fortunate One, the Time is ripe." Meral found herself being conducted through the archway of the Priests. Immediately a heavy stone door slid into place and Meral was alone with her conductor.

As her eyes became accustomed to the gloom, she perceived a snow-white donkey gorgeous with gold trappings. His hoofs were gold, his ears gold-tasselled and upon his back rested a seat of gold cloth and pearls. On the pummel were several strings of priceless pearls which the priest now removed and placed upon Meral, also a marvellous cloak of gold and a diadem of pearls. Bewildered, she was placed upon the donkey, which was then led up a long ramp of very shallow stone steps. They seemed never to get to the top. The bejewelled cloak was stiff with pearls, and heavily the diadem pressed upon her temples. Meral felt giddy with fright and strangeness. Then finally they emerged upon the roof of the Temple into the brilliant sun. Half blinded by the sudden change Meral could hardly keep her seat on the animal, so surprising it all seemed.

Awaiting her in full ceremonial robes and chanting a hymn to Ra, were a hundred priests ranged in two lines through which the white animal and the innocent maid, bedecked with gold and pearls, passed to the Little Temple on the Roof.

At the door, Meral was lifted from her gorgeous seat onto a silk rug and the officiating priest motioned for her to enter, alone. The door swung closed and Meral heard three bolts being shot into place.

She was alone in a small room of exquisite beauty. Silk tapestries hung upon the walls, thick silk rugs covered the floor. An intricate design of gold and blue and red had been applied on the ceiling, which was pierced in the centre by a slit two feet long by six inches wide. This opening was bevelled wider at the top and appeared to be cut in a solid block of stone. Directly under it, was a couch of ample proportions with carved Anubis-headed posts at the corners, and covered with rich

[228]

silken embroidery. Many cushions were piled upon it, and upon the floor. At the head and foot was an incense standard of carved gold and bronze in the form of a tripod, five feet high, holding a crystal dish from which heavy incense wove its spirals about the room.

There was no other furniture and no openings and no light, save the tiny oblong of sky visible above, which brought a soft light as of dawn. Not a sound broke the stillness. Meral kneeled by the divan and tried to compose her beating heart and startled senses.

A mood of deep exaltation crept over her. Her whole being seemed to expand. Laying aside the heavy cloak and diadem she prayed to the Great Ammon-Ra to accept her devotion. Soft, exquisite music now stole through the room. It seemed of Heaven. The incense grew stronger, as by magic more overpowering, and then before her appeared a god-like form in gold robes and flashing jewelled headdress.

Believing the vision to be the god incarnate, she threw herself at his feet in adoration.

A pair of bejewelled hands raised her and clasped her to a manly breast. It was assuredly real and human, this vision. With a shock, Meral realized this. But how did he get there, through solid walls?

Terrified, she struggled to be free and darted to the other side of the small room.

Her maiden conception of the Great God Ammon-Ra broke into a thousand fragments, as a bubble disperses from a blast of air, when Meral beheld the High Priest Rahotep divest his noble form of the gorgeous trappings of the god, and appear revealed in a soft white linen robe with a rich girdle of Tyrian silk embroidered

[229]

in gold. His body exhaled a perfume of amber and patchouli and sandal. The heavy odour seemed to fill the room, almost overpowering in its sensuous appeal. "Oh, Daughter of Man, chosen from all the common herd to this exalted office, thine is the great bliss of divine union, thine the knowledge of things ineffable. Upon thee will descend the favour of the greatest of all gods, the sublime, the glorious Ammon-Ra." The High Priest bowed three times while saying this.

"Come, Little One, I am the Servant of the Most High, through me will the Glorious One bestow his favours upon thee. Prepare thyself to receive His Glory. High Noon approaches and he will enter (casting his eyes to the aperture above) and bless thee." So saying Rahotep gently, but firmly, removed the gauze robes with which Meral had been draped by the Priestesses for the ceremony.

Meral tried to protest, but the inevitability of the ordeal to come and the authority and piercing eyes of the High Priest told her that resistance was useless. She was the lamb brought to the sacrificial altar. No struggle, no outcry would avail. Even Basadi, the Beloved, had watched her pass through the aisle of priests and made no move to save her.

Yet suddenly as her robes fell from her she made a despairing effort to escape. Gathering a garment about her, Meral slipped from the grasp of the High Priest and ran around the draped walls seeking an outlet in the hard granite of which they were built. The door six inches thick, was bolted and rigid.

Rahotep watched her graceful, though frantic, movements. His eyes were blazing, his breath coming quickly. Then with two strides, he was beside her. He gathered her into his powerful arms and with one sweep he placed her upon the couch just as a vivid ray of sunshine burst through the opening in the roof.

"The Glorious One greets thee!" Meral felt the hot breath of the Sun strike upon her. She heard music filling the little Temple on the Roof and a wild chant coming from she knew not where. It seemed to come from invisible voices and the High Priest Rahotep, murmuring a Ritual of Adoration of the Great God Ammon-Ra and of the glorious perfection of the Woman beneath its Rays, bent over her,—and the Ceremony of making Meral a Bride of the Sun, a Priestess of the Great Temple, soon drew to its close.

The vision faded away into the sunset. The Nile landscape again appeared and I was aware of the Poet approaching.

"How long have you been gone?" I asked. "Rather less than a half-hour," was the reply. So all this lifetime of emotion and adventure—for I have told but a fragment of it, was lived through in perhaps twenty minutes!

Small cause for wonder, however, as it had been another excursion into the fourth dimension, where Time is not.

The steamer tied up at Edfu during the night and the next morning at daybreak I was ready for a visit to the Temple dedicated to the Hawk-headed One, although as yet I did not know it was to be the Temple of the Vision. I thought I had confused it with the beautiful Temple of Dendereh over which I had thrilled the day before, although there were many sharp differences in construction between the Temple of My Memory and the Temple of my Vision. Owing to the midday heat all excursions were made at the beginning, or end of the day, and the Poet had declined this early jaunt. With perhaps a dozen energetic sightseers from the steamer, I was waiting for the dragoman to marshal the donkeys. By chance, or fate, what you will, I was the first mounted and, contrary to custom, the impulse seized me to ride ahead. Urging my donkey to a fast walk with the donkey boy behind, I proceeded through the town.

I had never been there before, but the memory of the vision the night before was so clear that I knew each turning necessary and, reaching the open road that led to the Temple, I urged the donkey into a gallop. I left the boy far behind, but I needed no guide. It was like going over roads long familiar. Arriving at the Temple façade, I was accosted by two Egyptian Police, for my pass to view the Temple. I explained that the party was just behind. Again, contrary to custom, for the native mind loves a little brief authority, I was allowed to enter, and alone.

And there I, in the flesh of a twentieth-century body, beheld the court of my vision of the evening before. The great outer court of the Acolytes where Meral, wearing the turquoise bracelet of identification, had bidden farewell to her parents and had danced before the High Priest.

One small person in this massive structure of stone! A grain of sand in the desert of eternity! I hurried with unhesitating steps, first through the Great Hall, then into the Inner Temple and yea, into the very Holy

of Holies itself, the Heart of the Secret Flame where
Meral had never been, where only the High Priests had
been allowed. A deep feeling of awe and sacrilege descended upon me.

Then hastening to the women's quarters I saw once
more the scenes of the vision, even the secret entrance to
the underground escape from the Temple to the town, a
tunnel two miles long.

How well I remember it in the vision! It was in the
middle of the Northern wall. This had been a sacred
part of the Temple and no curious eyes had been allowed ever to penetrate its mysteries. After following
a curving course for a mile or two, the secret passage
had come to an end in the cellar of a shop on the outskirts of the town near the Taran Well, a skilful piece
of engineering, which told of many years of arduous toil
for many slaves. Only a few of the high priests and
priestesses had known of its existence, and when it became necessary to repair it, the trained slaves had been
brought to a certain part outside, blindfolded, and released only at the spot needing repair, and when the
hours of labour were over, they had been again blindfolded and returned to a distant spot. Those who had
thought about it at all had assumed that this was some
passage under the temple, and thus the secret had been
kept for hundreds of years, as one generation of priests
and priestesses followed another. The entrance at either
end was guarded by a door which was opened and shut
by a peculiar contrivance which responded to a whispered word.

It was while supervising repair work on this tunnel
that Basadi had first met Meral near the Taran Well,

and it had also provided appointments for the many meetings that followed—and now, behold, here it was! —at least the entrance to it. How far it still went, I had no time to discover.

I hurried back to the main hall, for I must find the secret passage through which Meral had been conducted to the roof and the Temple of the Sun. With unerring footsteps I came upon it, in the centre of the South Wall of the Great Hall, the entrance now no longer concealed by draperies. Then I ascended with feverish haste the long stone ramp, built in the ten-foot wall of the Temple. Emerging upon the roof I rushed along, for now the party had arrived at the outer gate and my privacy would soon be broken. And half-way on that vast expanse of roofs, where a caravan of camels, donkeys and men could easily have lived their lives, I saw the object of my search, a stone-built one-story structure, about 20 feet square. The door being ajar, I entered. The room and the opening in the roof were the same, but alas! no draperies, no couch, no urns, only some dusty tools in one corner. But, with a deep thrill, I thought, "Now I must discover how the mysterious music had been produced and how the High Priest had so suddenly appeared from nowhere, upon the startled gaze of Meral." The building was fully 20 feet square but the chamber in which I stood was not more than 15 feet wide. Going outside, to the right of the door, I noticed an opening 2½ feet square which had evidently been closed by a block of stone, in days gone by. Getting down on my knees, regardless of dust, I peered in, then, unhesitatingly, *crawled* in. After 2 feet, which was the thickness of the wall, I could stand upright in a narrow passage, for that side of the Little Temple of the Sun had been built with a double wall. Half-way on the inner wall a block of stone 5 feet by 2 was hung on a pivot.

Through this, behind the embroidered hangings of the wall, had the High Priest entered. And at the end of the passage was a ledge upon which the musicians had sat, for the stone of the Temple wall in this corner had been bevelled out from 2 feet to the thickness of paper at the bottom edge, making an ideal sounding-board which produced the effect of the music being actually in the room!

Strange indeed were the emotions I experienced, standing there in that secret passage after a lapse of two thousand years, as my mind grasped the clever, but entirely natural, means used to overwhelm the reason and paralyse the will of an evolving soul—a soul which had been clothed in a beautiful body, the lure of which had aroused the ardour of a dominant personality, for Rahotep had made his will law to the thousands who had come under his influence. Strangely confusing was the reality of the twentieth century, combined with the occult and the ancient rituals. The mind is an unplumbed reservoir of forgotten things, and truth may be found at the bottom of the well.

The party, now arriving on the roof, saw an excited, dusty female emerging from a hole in the wall and marvelled at the archaeological enthusiasm thus displayed. But she . . . put on her Oriental look and said nothing.

BOOK IV

TRAVEL SIDE-LIGHTS

APPENDIX A

IN the swing around the globe, few places hold the imagination more than Egypt, the Land of the Pharaohs. It combines the lure of antiquity with the comforts of modern life. It is the Happy Hunting Ground of unattached females, although luxurious travel facilities have made Egypt possible even for the Tired Business Man. The ways and means of such a trip must be considered sooner or later, and of dollars, only, will there be need in this bill of Egyptian Travel. No cents, added and multiplied, will enter into the picture.

The voyage for two from New York to Alexandria, taking in the delightful Mediterranean Cruise and stopping for a nibble at many fascinating places, can be done strictly first-class for $800 plus $200 for incidentals, that is, a thousand dollars; or it can cost four thousand—the difference depending largely upon the steamer accommodations and private excursions.

A four-months trip for two, taking in Italy and France on the way home, will represent a minimum of $4000, although it would be quite easy to spend double or treble this amount. This means stopping at the best hotels, with first-class rail accommodation, and comfortable, but not the best, steamer accommodations. It might be done for less (indeed thousands yearly do it for much less, but not "comfortably") and one's letter of credit should represent at least another thousand for emergencies, and the unexpected. Here should be noted a word of advice for the Business Man—be sure to take several hundred dollars in Travellers' Checks—and to have a portion of that sum put into separate books, one for each member of the party, and payable to his or her signature.

Your wife or daughter should have a thousand dollars in Travellers' Checks put away for emergencies and not spent—unless she has her own letter of credit, when a few hundreds will do. This is a wise precaution against sudden illness or, indeed, a death. Two cases will illustrate—: A very wealthy man with a letter of credit of $50,000 was travelling with his wife in Italy. Motoring in an out-of-the-way place on the Lakes, he was seized with a heart attack and put to bed in a little roadside hotel. In the shock of the occurrence his wife did not think about money until she needed to send the hired car to the next town for medical assistance and supplies. The driver refused to go without money. Her husband's bill case had been stolen. He had always attended to the finances. She had $1.35 in her purse. To be sure he had a letter of credit representing thousands, but useless to his wife. The limited credit that the inn accorded to strangers was soon exhausted. The man died. The distracted wife had not money enough to send a cable, not even a telegram.

She was dependent upon the charity of the local doctor and banker, who were not disposed to be generous. One of them even asked for her marriage certificate. He remarked that, "there are so many strange couples going

APPENDIX A

motoring through here." Money and friends were ultimately available, but the agonized wife had much unnecessary humiliation, added to her grief.

Another and a commoner case was that of a wealthy
man from Chicago. He and his wife were both equipped
with a thousand dollars in Travellers' Checks but they
were spending money freely and, as it was very convenient
to pay by these checks, which are legal tender practically
everywhere, their supply was soon exhausted. The
gentleman took a two-day's trip to Belgium, leaving his
wife in Paris. On Saturday, the day he had expected to
return, she received a wire that he had been detained
for three days longer. The wife found herself alone in
a strange city without money. The bank where her husband had a letter of credit was closed till Monday and
the hotel manager had already supplied her with cash,
so that she did not like to ask him for more. The same
pride prevented her borrowing from the few friends she
knew in Paris. For the first time in her life she was
concerned for the need of a dollar. She spent the day
miserably in her room and registered a vow that from
that time on she would be supplied with a personal
financial background—and that a Letter of Credit, as
well as Travellers' Checks, would be added to her list of
necessities for the next trip.

Alexandria holds few travellers. Their Mecca is
Cairo, and the Shepheard's Hotel—who has not heard
of it? On its broad terrace eddies a ceaseless flow of
cosmopolitan life and from its vantage ground can be
seen, filing past in the street, a continuous procession of
the picturesque Egyptian scenes. People will extol the
virtues of the Semiramis, recently built on the bank of the

Nile, its comforts and exclusiveness, but few "tourists doing a first time" will regret having selected the older hostelry with its mixture of Eastern and Western atmosphere.

The caravan life, especially, is a game to be played by those who are travelling on the sunny side of fifty dollars per day. One reads of the adventures and the thrills of caravaning. These may, or may not, come one's way; but "what it will cost" is as certain to interest every traveller as the unchangeable facts of sky, wind, sand and sun. So is the Weekly Hotel Bill. One of these (see page 244), selected at random, from Shepheard's Hotel, shows the "bare bones" of living for two in a commodious double room and luxurious bathroom—at the "best hotel" in Cairo, Luxor or Assouan. Tips, laundry and valet raises the bill to twenty-five dollars a day, and, of course, incidentals and shopping are what one makes them. Expenses for sightseeing, such as motors, carriages, mosque and tomb fees, guide, camel and donkey hire, plus tips, when one is actively sightseeing, double this amount.

A compartment for two in the sleeping-car from Cairo to Luxor costs $60, all told, just for over-night; whereas the guide's charge on the railroad was only 20 piastres or $1.00. But Shehata, our dragoman, went third class in the native car and slept on a wooden seat all night. He could not have travelled on that particular *train de luxe* except as our "servant."

He bobbed up serenely at the station at Luxor the next morning, ready to corral the necessary "boys" to help us off with the luggage. A friend—Shehata had a genuine gift for producing one whenever convenient—had already appeared and taken his bag—a very smart kit bag, by the way, of English sole leather—and would arrange for his lodgings and thus leave him free to attend to "his Ladies."

It should be here stated that it is not in the least necessary, if one is familiar with Egyptian travel, to take a guide permanently. Shehata could easily have been dismissed at Cairo and a Luxor guide engaged, and the same at Assouan. But the extra cost was trifling and we preferred to stick to the ills that we knew of than to fly to evils that we knew not of.

Travel on the "accommodation" trains is slow and expensive, over double the present rates in America.

To go from Luxor to Edfu is 66 miles. It took from 6:20 A. M. to 10:40 A. M., only about sixteen miles an hour. A first-class ticket costs one pound (nearly five dollars normal exchange). The fast train makes the distance in 2½ hours with supplement, that is, extra fare, which averages about four dollars an hour per person. One usually has the added expense of a dragoman who goes second-class at ten shillings, so that a little trip up the river for the day represents:

2 persons and guide on the Railroad	$25.
3 donkeys	4.
Lunch carried with you in a basket	5.
Carriages	2.
	$36.

The same thing could be done from New York to Trenton for $18.

The dragoman's fee is extra and runs from 20 to 75 piastres a day ($1 to $3.75), average 50 to 60 piastres.

A WOMAN TENDERFOOT IN EGYPT

The best hotels—such as Shepheards at Cairo—The Winter Palace at Luxor—The Cataract at Assouan—have fixed charges:

Pension:

Breakfast	Piastre 20
Lunch	40
Dinner	60

120 piastres, or $6 a day per person

Rooms:

Two beds, very nice	Piastres 100 = $5.00
Private bathrooms are about £2, viz.	$8.00.
A room and private bath and board per day for one,	$20.
For two sharing room	$28.
Add tips for four room attendants and three dining-room	3.

Total, per day, about $32.

Trips and excursions will cost quite
$20 per day for two . . . . .   .   20.

Total, per day, about $52.

These figures provide for comfortable, first-class travel, with everything one wants, but not for private sitting rooms, nor extravagances, nor purchases of souvenirs. Of course if one can travel leisurely, the average day excursions will cost less. One can travel on the Nile in a *dahabeyeh*, the native small passenger boat, propelled by steam and wind, for the same average expense.

In a "Cook's party" I believe Egypt can be done as low as $10 or $12 a day—and pleasantly done, too, by steamer and comfortable hotels, and "seeing the sights."

APPENDIX A

A *felucca*, the boat with the long swallow tails for sails, can be hired for two or three dollars for an evening on the Blue Nile—the boatmen love to sing at their tasks and the weird strains blend harmoniously with the brilliant sunset fading beyond the Tombs of the Kings at Luxor or, if one is far enough South to see it, at Assouan, with the fiery Southern Cross.

It is the hour of witchery, when the intimate African night embraces the day. New York, and London, seem so far in the future that one idly wonders if they really exist. Calmed and soothed, one returns to the luxurious hotel and slips inside the white canopied fly-flea-net and dreams of the next day's delights.

Shehata's expense account rendered during one of our trips in 1922 shows that the H. C. L. has struck Egypt quite as effectively as other countries where the minority of men and women travel, and the majority travail. It covered a period of two weeks and represented those incidental expenses for which I had not paid cash at the time.

This bill, which totalled about $90., was a trick bill. Every time I added it up, I got another result. So did the typist, who copied it. So did the Poet, the delightful woman who travelled with me. We finally decided that Shehata's figures were as nearly correct as any of ours.

I had Shehata about a month and his daily expenses averaged $4.00, for general guiding service. This represented wages and transportation, by train, tram, carriage, canal, or donkey. (No food or lodging). He was on duty as many hours a day as the needs, or whim, of the employer, dictated. A guide for desert trips is more expensive, and one for a few days only would average more. A present is always expected at the termination of service. The giving of gifts, especially among the Bedouins, who are a wild, free, race, and affect to despise the degraded town folk, is an Oriental custom not to be ignored. Ten years ago, before the Great War, on my first caravan trip which had been a profitable one to him, Shehata presented me with a new striped satin *galabeyeh,* the native flowing robe, for which he had paid the equivalent of fifty dollars. He was always very well-dressed in the long satin robes with an over-robe of heavy silk, pongee or white; and above that an outer garment of blue broadcloth bound in silk. A Bedouin turban, a Malacca cane which he carried as a badge of office, American shoes of tan leather, kept well-polished, and a voluminous silk scarf, completed his picturesque attire. The scarf of heavy, white, soft silk had long fringe especially knotted and was worn in many ways, usually thrown twice around the neck, the long ends flapping in the breeze. Sometimes it completely covered the head and shoulders to protect them from the sun and wind—that sharp desert wind that penetrates to the very marrow. Sometimes, with a grand gesture, it was spread over a stone on the ground for Milady to sit upon and protect her light garments from the dirt—the dirt, the omnipresent dirt—around the habitations of the lower classes. But though in the neighbourhood of villages, everything is dirty, out in the free desert all is clean and pure and wind-swept. Pitiless, if you like, in its immensity for those who are not desert-bred. But a conquered giant for this son of a Bedouin Sheik in whose brain stirs the consciousness of unnumbered Children of the Desert.

APPENDIX A

Camping with a caravan costs four to eight pounds a day per person (average at least $30). A three-days' trip into the desert for two, costs a minimum of $200. For a week it is cheaper, a minimum of $260, as everything, the animals, boys, tents, etc., is engaged by the week. There will be personal extras such as table water, wine, cigars, which, as always, depend upon the tastes and pocket-books of the caravaners. That it is worth whatever it costs is the opinion of most travellers in the desert. A competent dragoman lifts every atom of responsibility off one's mind and provides camels, riding-dromedaries, donkeys, tents, beds, chairs, tables, linen, china, silver and food to the point of luxury. The desert heat-fierceness of noon stirs one to battle, and the desert peace of night and morning wraps around the charmed soul and comfortable body and one feels less a slave and more a King, of being at one with the Maker of all things who ever finds expression in the vasty spaces of the sand and sky. Try it, O jaded One!

A Monument Ticket is necessary for Upper Egypt, which admits one to all the principal tombs and temples, which have been closed so that a fee may be extracted from the visiting public. The ticket is good for the season and costs 120 Egyptian piastres, which at the rate of exchange in 1922 was under five dollars. At normal exchange it would be six. It is interesting to note that my ticket was dated, good till June 30, 1915, and a rubber stamp brought the date up to 1922. It is one of the many reminders of the Great War. All tourist travel ceased a few months after Germany ruthlessly razed through Belgium and started the world conflagration that still smoulders, amid the ruins of monarchies and the rickety bodies of young republics.

The first Mediterranean trip of the Adriatic in 1922, which landed us, the Poet and I with several hundred other "tourists," was the first of the kind since 1915, and the Monument Ticket had lain idle for seven long years because of the Great War.

It is also interesting to note that the language upon it was French and Arabic. The French language is used largely as a medium of communication between the natives and the resident foreign population of Greeks, Italians, Syrians, as well as French. It is also the diplomatic language, and the one used among the upper classes of Egypt. The French Consul at Luxor is a native Copt, speaking no English. In the Italian Consulate at Cairo I met only native clerks, speaking French. The *commercial* foreign language is English, also the "official" language which means that of the. Anglo-Egyptian government.

In Cairo one could live for the rest of one's life in the English colony and never require a foreign word. But shift, ever so little, into the Cairean Society and one is deaf and dumb without French; and without a smattering of Arabic, one cannot hope to get at the psychology of the common people. True, with a little observation one can tell whether the native is lying or not—for into his face comes the subtle Oriental look. It is not so much an expression as the absence of an expression. A native handles the truth not as an immutable fact but as plastic convenience. Many questions asked by the Occidental strike the differently trained mind of the Oriental as unnecessary, or impertinent. "How many children have you, Shehata, and how many wives?"

asked a friend of mine as he was being conducted through the garden of Roda Island—the same garden, if tradition be true, where the infant Moses was cradled in the bulrushes. Remnants of its vanished glories are still to be seen.

The voice of Shehata, excessively smooth, answered this important business man from America without an instant's hesitation.

"I have nine children, Sir, and four wives."

"Good, good, fancy that, you rascal," my friend replied delightedly.

Turning to Shehata, my surprise subsided. His face was emptied of all intelligence, as he motioned with his usual sweeping bow, the direction we were to take.

Later when out of hearing, I asked,

"Shehata, why did you lie to my friend?"

"Ah, no, Madam, that was not a lie. Why should I tell him that I have two children and one wife? He give me bad blood when he ask. No man asks about the family of another man. It is bad. I tell him what I think he like to know."

"That is some husky, handsome devil you've got for a dragoman," commented my friend, as we stood at one end of the flat-bottomed barge used as a ferry from Roda Island to the mainland. "But I like him—and he seems respectable. I guess he is all right."

The barge gave a sudden lurch as the current struck it and I sat down involuntarily, upon a pile of lumber. My friend landed upon a basket of onions and the subject of Shehata and his family was a closed incident between us.

To get back to the "How Much" of it, this gentleman

was "seeing Egypt" at an average cost of $150 a day which included a private motor car, a wife and a maid—a dragoman, 3 rooms and 2 baths. He could have had a small *dahabeyeh* in place of the motor car for the same amount. Motors are well enough around Cairo, but of no use in Upper Egypt, as there are no roads suitable for them. They are quite out of the picture also. But that would deter few motor fans, and, doubtless, the time will come when the harried tourist will do "from Cairo to Assouan" and back, taking five-minute stops at the temples and tombs, in three days instead of the three weeks now allowed for the Cook's tour. And, sinking into his berth on the steamer at Alexandria utterly fagged with indigestion, both mental and physical, he will say, "I wonder why people make such a fuss about Egypt. It is a country of the dead; and the people who are alive are a dirty lot."

We can vision what will happen to this motor tourist, for, even now, one meets his kind on the Nile steamers. The motor tourists of the future will have seen nothing of the cultivated, civilized, but picturesque, home life of the modern upper classes. At the hotels they will have met their fellow travellers and a set of servants and guides who are organized to take care of them. They will have seen a few side-shows trumped up for the tourist. They will have bought some metal shawls at Assuit, where the caravan trails cross from the Arabian and the Libyan Deserts. They will have paid $6 for one and $18 for the other—a beauty! Some embroideries and mummy jewelry at Luxor will have been added to the collection—$30. or $40. more gone. Some beads and shell necklaces made by the Sudanese at

APPENDIX A

Assouan, bought for "nothing at all," perhaps $5 for the lot; and several will be given away, grandly, to Mrs. Smith and Mrs. Jones of the party. They will have dashed into the bazaars again at Cairo and picked up that purple silk *galabeyeh*, shot with gold threads, for $15, as they could get nothing cheaper "up the River"— and it will be just the thing for Mamie: she can add some fur and make an evening wrap of it. They will have done tombs and temples, until nothing but a real "humdinger" will be able to budge them off the seat of the motor. They will prefer to sit comfortably, take a glimpse of the outside and check it off on the list as "done." When that time comes, may the shades of Anubis, the God of the Underworld, rise up and swallow them!

If one has any business, or writing to do, it will be well to carry a typing machine. Stenography and type-writing in English is very difficult to obtain and the following bill shows that one "pays by the nose":

J. STEINHART
1 hour's work in room		Pt 35.
9½ double space pages at Pt 7		66.5
2½ single ditto at Pt 1o		25
12 carbons at Pt 1		12.
		Pt 138.5
Balance PT 1oo		
3 pages single space @ Pt 1o	30.	
3 carbons @ Pt 1	3.	133.
		PT 271.5

A WOMAN TENDERFOOT IN EGYPT

Feb. 19th 1922

Dear Mrs. Seton, I have *managed as a favor to get this* done on one of the machines in the Hotel, so thought you would like to have it straight away.

Yours truly,
J. Steinhart.

This represents dictation, reading rough notes, and copying corrected MSS. of the same, for a newspaper article of 3000 words, for which, with ordinary press rates, a journalist would receive perhaps $30. $13.50 for clerical work is over 43% of the whole, which leaves $16.50 for an article which cost a thousand dollars to get and argues a certain amount of brains and style, or it would not have been accepted for publication at all. The position of the author versus the operator becomes a *reductio ad absurdum.*

When I asked this intelligent English girl why her charges were so high, she seemed surprised. She stated that most people expected to make enough in the winter during the tourist season not to have to work all summer!

In studying my note-books of ten years ago it is evident that the God of Change and Circumstance has Egypt in charge, so far as the "How Much" of it is concerned. The price of everything the traveller needs, or wants, is from four to six times higher.

I am dealing only, with the independent traveller, who chooses not to plan her trip but to trust to the God of Incident to guide her peregrinations and to decide the What, When, and Where of it.

Any one wishing to travel in Egypt as cheaply, and

Crown 8vo.   xxvi + 874 pp.   21s. net.   Postage 9d.

EGYPTIAN ANTIQUITIES IN THE NILE VALLEY

A DESCRIPTIVE HANDBOOK

BY

JAMES BAIKIE, D.D., F.R.A.S.

With 61 Illustrations and 106 Plans

This book is an attempt to describe consecutively and in a readable way the existing examples of Egyptian architecture and art that are to be found on the ancient sites in the Nile Valley, from Alexandria to Meroë, near Khartum. The great temples, pyramids, and tombs of Memphis, Thebes, etc., with their lesser companions, are treated with sufficient fullness of detail to render their structure and ornamentation intelligible to the layman ; while special attention is directed to the outstanding examples of Egyptian sculpture and painting, and to the most notable specimens of the matchless Egyptian craftsmanship to be found in, for example, the Cairo Museum.

ORDER FORM

To..
    Bookseller
    ....

    ....

    Please send me...............*copies of* ' EGYPTIAN ANTI-
QUITIES IN THE NILE VALLEY ', *by* JAMES BAIKIE, D.D.,
F.R.A.S. (21s. *net*), *for which I enclose*..............................

        (*Signed*) ....

            ....

            ....

Date..............................

Methuen & Co. Ltd., 36 Essex Street, London, W.C.2

[P.T.O.

Crown 8vo.   xxvi + 874 pp.   21s. net.   Postage 9d.

EGYPTIAN ANTIQUITIES IN THE NILE VALLEY

A DESCRIPTIVE HANDBOOK

BY

JAMES BAIKIE, D.D., F.R.A.S.

With 61 Illustrations and 106 Plans

THE GREAT SPHINX

Methuen & Co. Ltd., 36 Essex Street, London, W.C.2

[P.T.O.

see a great deal, as quickly and as comfortably as possible, will find himself or herself drifting to the nearest office of Thomas Cook & Son, as this service is, to the traveller in Egypt, a Common Sense side-light.

Speaking of that very desirable attribute, common sense, this is a good place to comment upon the silly woman and her silly guide. One frequently hears stories of a woman falling somewhat under the influence of her dragoman. The whole system is so foreign to her home surroundings that she fails to get her bearings immediately and allows the gorgeously clothed gentleman, who is handling her money and giving her all sorts of information, more or less accurate, to presume upon her ignorance and good nature and assume the place of a friend, rather than a servant. She has not hesitated to invite him to take tea with her, or a meal at a restaurant, or to sit beside her on terms of equality in a carriage or motor.

A good dragoman is entitled to all respect for his efficiency and accomplishments, and one should feel thankfully appreciative for the valuable services he renders one—when he does render them.

But it is hard to understand the sweeping aside of conventions and prejudices, both social and racial, which would permit a friendly intimacy. That this has been done occasionally there is no question.

It has seemed to me in the cases which have come under personal observation that these anomalies arise more from a lack of social standards than from a lack of morals. And it is absurd to imply that when an English Madam takes a caravan into the desert that she is lured there by the charms of any dusky Adonis. There is a

type of Englishwoman who can go anywhere, any time,
with impunity. She is a seasoned traveller and she fears
not any man. This leaves a very small percentage of
silly women of whom a clever, educated Arab, can make
fools—and about whom occasional grotesque stories
centre.

APPENDIX B

THE Oldest World Courier, is the House of Cook, and its history reads like a Romance of Business.

The story was told to me by the present senior member, Mr. Frank H. Cook, mostly over our coffee while the Adriatic was speeding her way through calm seas on the last lap from Naples to Alexandria, and I give it as an interesting side-light on Egyptian travel, for, to the tourist, Egypt and Thomas Cook & Son are Siamese Twins.

Though a courteous and pleasing personality with clear blue eyes that look at you kindly, Mr. Cook has all the Englishman's horror of "rushing into print"—personal publicity being his pet abomination.

During several conversations Mr. Cook warmed to his topic, however, and eventually delivered himself of the following array of facts, told in a low, musical voice which produces its words in a leisurely fashion. There is no sense of hurry or stress about this gentleman who has done his share to carry on one of the most interesting businesses in the world. He is the typical well-set-up, well-groomed Englishman, in the late fifties; grey moustache and hair with an American tendency to scantiness. He was made a C. I. E. (Commander of the Order of the Indian Empire) in 1896; is a Knight of Grace of the Order of St. John of Jerusalem, and one of His Maj-

esty's Lieutenants for the City of London, and lives at
Barnett Hill, Wonersh, Guildford.

Thomas Cook & Son came into being because of a
necessity, which had not even been realized, as it had
"never been done," and one knows what that means in
England. But when the trail was blazed, there was an
increasing stream of people who wanted to travel over it
until now the trademark of the business is the world with
a band of "Cook's Travel Service" girdling its circum-
ference.

It is not so much the interesting tale of persistency in
overcoming difficulties, nor even of dealing with nation
after nation, unaccustomed to modern methods of travel,
that makes the recital of this business a romance. Many
an enterprise can record such, but it is the Aladdin-like
possibilities it has created for the inexperienced, as well
as the experienced, traveller, that makes the record
unique. The old maid in Wisconsin, the school teacher
in Maine, the elderly couple in Ohio, who had never been
out of their home town and never would have adventured,
had not Thomas Cook & Son been within reach to take
them courteously by the hand, and to teach them the
A. B. C.'s of seeing how other people live, and where;
and to take off their shoulders all necessity for learning
the X. Y. Z. of travel. Likewise the seasoned globe-trot-
ter and the business man, seeking new fields of endeav-
our, no less than the ordinary traveller for pleasure and
recreation, whether men or women, old or young, have all
alike found in the House of Cook a "guide, philosopher
and friend." For all, the "Man from Cook's" has relieved many a difficulty and brought peace to the
troubled mind.

APPENDIX B

No one factor is in any degree so responsible for the tremendous increase of travel as this institution. It has shown one-half of the world how the other half lives and by the bond of common knowledge who shall say that it has not helped towards the good-will of all people?

"It all started back in 1841," said the present senior member. "Thomas Cook, my grandfather, was much interested in the temperance cause and conceived the idea of bringing a great number of people from Leicester to the town of Loughborough to a big temperance fête which was being organized on a beautiful estate about twenty miles from Leicester. So he arranged for a special train to go to Loughborough on the Midland Railroad. The third-class fare was one shilling and he established this as the excursion rate. The affair was a great success and it was not long before Thomas Cook was asked to do another excursion.

"It was the very first time that any organization had been made to handle the public at a minimum fixed price to and from definite points, and was the beginning of the tremendous business which now runs today into every civilized corner of the globe. An amusing instance of British conservatism is found in the fact that the shilling fare, 3rd class, established on the occasion of this first public excursion, remained until the outbreak of the war as the excursion rate between Loughborough and Leicester."

After Mr. Thomas Cook had managed several of these excursions, he saw the possibility in the idea as a business and arrange the first Tour to Scotland. It was about 1847, before there was any through rail going between England and Scotland. The tourists were taken to Fleetwood by train, then by steamer to Glasgow. The occasion was thought to be so remarkable an event that public receptions were given in the Town Hall to the travellers by the Provosts of Glasgow and Edinburgh. Guns were fired and bands of music provided an escort.

From England and Scotland Mr. Cook turned his attention to the Continent, with equal success, and in addition to the arranging of personally-conducted parties, the business of independent tickets for travel by railroad and steamship, now so important a branch of the business, particularly in America, was developed.

The Information Department, the Banking and Exchange Department, the Mail Department, and all the multifarious branches of the World-Wide Travel Service, came as natural sequence.

"Then from the Continent," continued the Senior member, "we extended to Palestine in 1868; in 1872 my grandfather arranged and escorted the first 'Tour Around the World,' and about the same time the firm established offices in New York."

Although both Thomas Cook and his father, John M. Cook, had previously visited the United States, it was the success with which the firm in 1871 managed the tour to Europe of a large delegation of American Freemasons—a body of prominent Knights Templar—that led to the opening of a "Cook's Office" in New York, and subsequently in Boston, Philadelphia, San Francisco, and other large cities of the United States and Canada, and the development of the present large American organization. In the half-century that has elapsed this has become a very important branch of the business and its relations with the American public increasingly intimate and cordial.

APPENDIX B

It was in 1870 that John Mason Cook went to Egypt and chartered from the Egyptian Government the first public steamer for the trip up the Nile. He obtained from the Khedive the exclusive control of it, and of the other steamers which it was necessary to get in order to take care of the increasing demand.

Then, after the military expeditions of 1882 and 1884, the steamers were no longer available for private travel after having transported all the troops, and the Cook firm proceeded to build its own fleet of steamers.

In 1914 they had twenty steamers on the Nile. The British Government took over ten of them to go out to Mesopotamia during the Great War to transport the Red Cross personnel and Hospital service.

The service on the Nile was re-established in the winter of 1920–21 with the remaining ten steamers and two others which had to be added soon.

"Have you any equipment left in Jerusalem?" was my next question.

"Not very much; the Turks collared all our camp equipment and saddles there."

The next big move after Egypt for the firm was to establish themselves in India about 1878; then came Australia and New Zealand. South Africa was brought into the general travelling world in 1890 and then the trail of travel facilities was extended into the far East, China, and Japan, in 1900, and the girdle of the Cook's banner around the world was complete.

How many people realized that the great increase of world pleasure travel from the days of our grandfathers is largely due to this enterprise carried on by three generations?

A WOMAN TENDERFOOT IN EGYPT

Today the London office in Ludgate Circus has a personnel of about 1300 with 600 in the accountant staff; and 3500 men and women are numbered on the permanent staff of the business. There are 150 offices forming nuclei from which flow the streams of travellers into all the various countries, Russia alone being as yet unsupplied with the service.

The ramifications of this business are tremendous, and the Cook Continental Time Table may be cited as an example of what now seems a simple piece of literature, but which necessitated a wide knowledge to create.

Beside the tale of daily difficulties overcome and thousands of individuals assisted, there are several high lights that stand out in the long history of this business of transportation.

There are the stories of the 1884 and 1885 expeditions into Egypt and the Sudan; the Jerusalem expedition when the Kaiser, then at the height of his glory, travelled royally to Palestine; and of the effort to correct abuses and to modernize travel in India.

About this last, when Mr. Frank Cook was asked what was the most interesting feature in his personal business career, the reply came rather whimsically: "The most interesting and successful thing I personally put through, perhaps, should not be counted, as it was ultimately a failure: but the British Government asked us to go into India and see what we could do to assist the travellers going to Mecca. The Pilgrims to Mecca had to go from Bombay by steamers to Jeddah and then from that point it was about 40 miles to Mecca. Of course, none but Mahomedans were allowed in Mecca and very few were able to get as far as Jeddah. The crowd of Pilgrims would congregate at Bombay, and much hardship was endured because of the limited accommodations in the steamers. The Steamship Companies had no fixed fare but charged as much as circumstances and the pocket-book of the Pilgrims would permit. Great extortion and abuse had grown up.

"We succeeded in establishing a fixed fare on steamer transportation and made that part of India a much more possible place in which to travel, but we could not do more without the monopoly and the British Government had only granted a subsidy and we could not compete to get travel into really proper condition.

"Now, I am afraid conditions have gone back pretty much, as it was no use to continue under the circumstances."

The story of the Jerusalem expedition under John M. Cook gives an idea of what can be done with the monopoly of the travelling facilities.

"In 1898 my father happened to be at Vesuvius when the Emperor was making the journey. You know we operate a railroad to the summit. And the Emperor was so pleased with our arrangements that he told my father of his intention to go to Palestine and asked if he would handle the entire expedition. When the time came I was sent over to Hamburg and saw the Hof-Master and made the preliminary arrangements. It was a much-heralded affair.

"The Emperor had nearly 250 people in his immediate suite and travelled like a Hohenzollern, and there were all the Pashas and Turkish officials and people responsible for the expedition. Altogether we took care of about 600 people, the largest party that had gone to Jerusalem since the time of the crusades. We swept the country of horses and carriages, and almost of food, but the people were happy with the gold left behind."

"It must have been rather trying for the independent travellers," was my comment.

"The *Emperor* was travelling. Why, they knocked down part of the wall beside the Jaffa Gate so that the Empress could *drive* into Jerusaem. The Empress rode in. I could not help comparing the difference in the entrance of General Allenby, who, as conqueror of Palestine, was content to walk through this historic gate on foot."

Perhaps the most notable achievement of this business which started so modestly in the middle of the last century was the response the firm was able to make to the British Government for assistance and facilities in transporting the entire British Expeditionary Forces into Egypt and the Sudan in 1884 and again in 1885.

"Late in the Autumn of 1881, I think it was, my father was sent for by His Royal Highness the Duke of Cambridge, who was Commander-in-Chief of the British Army. Lord Wolseley (then Sir Garnet), Minister of War, was also present.

"The Duke said: 'You know more of Egypt than any other man, Mr. Cook,' and then he asked my father which was the better route to transport the troops that Lord Wolseley wished to send to Egypt to quell the rebellion, the Red Sea route or the Nile route.

"My father replied: 'It is against my interest, your Highness, but I think the Red Sea route is the better one of the two.'

"There were glances exchanged between the Duke and

APPENDIX B

Lord Wolseley. You see, the latter favoured the Nile route and his counsel ultimately prevailed. My father was asked to handle the transportation of the troops and this was done by carrying whale-boats which had been supplied by England and transported on British ships to Alexandria, where they were put on board the Cook's steamers together with the troops and the entire equipment necessary and taken up the Nile to Wadi Halfa.

"From there the troops proceeded in the small boats and a body of them had to travel across the desert from Korti to Metemmeh."

These few brief sentences, told so simply, outlined one of the most strenuous expeditions ever staged.

In 1885 Cook's handled the transportation of the second British Expeditionary Force of 7000 men sent out by Lord Wolseley to rescue General Gordon, and, again in 1898, when Kitchener's army again had to march on to Khartoum.

This, in a nut shell, gives a few suggestions of what a private enterprise can accomplish in patriotic service to its country.

The History of the Great War, so fresh in all our minds, holds many thrilling stories of similar service to country, but, again, the House of Cook can be credited with having been the pioneer.

During the war, owing to its world contact, the Cook firm was able to supply a great deal of information to the Government and had the honour of being publicly thanked in the House of Parliament for the very great services it had rendered in many channels and especially at the outbreak of hostilities in aiding travellers to get home. Splendid work was done by some of the various

European Cook's offices to relieve distress and to furnish money and even the food, necessary for life. People who never had had a day's worry about physical comfort found themselves stranded without the usual medium of exchange. The bright yellow gold had lost for the moment its purchasing power. For example the office at Carlsbad, after two weeks of the war, at last managed to get through a special train on which hundreds of miserable travellers who had drifted to Carlsbad were sent to the seaport; also Cook's was able to collect most of their effects.

"Even in London," said Mr. Cook, "I remember how difficult matters were. There was one of the big bankers of New York, a man controlling millions, who begged, as a personal favour, a cheque cashed for £50, and he was very glad to get it too."

The Vienna office was opened all through the war in a curious way. It was commandeered to maintain a certain part of the activity of travel and Cook's was compelled to take an area and to do the usual ticket business for that area.

Mr. Frank Cook has been to America a number of times and last year spent a week end in New York, from Friday until Tuesday, which sounds sufficiently like American business methods to please our most enterprising "boosters." Mr. Cook has further testified to his appreciation of America by marrying Miss Beatrice Lindell of St. Louis, Missouri, in 1894. There is one daughter, Frances Beatrice, now 24 years old, who is described as an "out door girl," who plays the cello very well, and who is not likely to assume a business career and carry on the business of her progenitors.

APPENDIX B

Of the morale side of the business Mr. Frank Cook said: "Our aim of the House, is to give the travelling public the best possible service and to develop travel. We have training classes and language classes for our staff. The principal difficulty we have, of course, is to get the right man who speaks both English and the language of the country."

I asked Mr. Cook what would be his method if he wished to establish the firm in Timbuctoo and he replied: "I should go to the local railroad administration and say that it would be for our mutual benefit, as it would develop traffic, etc., and ask them to give us facilities.

"We always use our own people who have been trained and these men use as far as possible the local people in unimportant positions.

"Our office force which comes into contact with the public, works on a salary and a percentage of the business each one does.

"The women clerks taken on during the war have given good service and are very valuable, but the difficulty with employing women in the more responsible positions is that the job takes long and special training and just when a woman is nicely trained she is apt to marry. So we use them more in the clerical branches.

"We have found," continued Mr. Cook, "that the ex-service man in seeking re-employment is not satisfied with what he got before the war. Many of them are married and they demand £400, instead of the £200 formerly paid, on the ground that they cannot live on less.

"In fact the salary list has more than doubled the pre-war prices. To be sure there are offsets which tend to balance this cost of operation, such as the increase in fares by the railroads and transportation lines, and the raising of monetary values all along the scale.

"The cost of travelling has greatly increased. The number of travellers has not increased, and they are very largely Americans."

Here, I suggested that the reason for this was not only because there was more loose cash in the United States, but because many felt like the young man of eighteen, living in a Missouri hamlet, who was taken by his father to the market town twenty miles away. The horses were lame, so the boy for the first time was transported on the railroad and also for the first time visited what, to him, was a great Metropolis of 2,000 persons. He saw a one-ring circus and had dinner at the two-story Hotel. On the return journey he was very quiet, his father asked him what was troubling him, and he said, "Father, I've been thinkin' that travellin' is a great educator."

Interesting late developments of the business are the motor-car and the aëroplane services, at present more important abroad than in the United States. For this servant of the public, like the courier, leads while it serves.

"More persons," said Mr. Cook, "wanted to fly across the Channel last summer than we at any one time had accommodations for. The Air Service between London and Paris has become most popular."

Here we shall leave the House of Cook, which, starting in a small local philanthropic movement over eighty years ago, has extended its helping hand around the world, and is now safely taking the traveller off into space.

THE END

SEKHMET
The Lion-headed Goddess in the
Temple of Mat, Luxor

SEKHMET
The Lion-headed Goddess in the
Temple of Ptah

[267]

ON THE NILE RIVER

"The style of this river craft has not changed since the Pharaohs. . . . Over the bridge, however, roll modern freight and passenger cars."

Saphia Zaghloul
Le Caire 22 Février 1922

Madame Saad Zaghlul Pasha draped in El Watan, the Red and
White Flag of Egypt

EGYPTIAN LADIES' DEMONSTRATION
The first ever staged in Cairo

THE LADIES' DELEGATION OF INDEPENDENCE
Protesting against the Exile of Zaghlul Pasha, Martial Law, etc.

EGYPTIAN LADY
Wearing the *Habara* and *Boukra*

MADAME NIFT RATIB PASHA
Member of the "Ladies' Wafd"

MLLE. MARY MARCOS HANNA

MLLE. AÏDA MARCOS HANNA

MADAME RIAD FANOUS
Member of "La Femme Nouvelle"

MADAME WACYF BEY BOUTROS GHALI
Member of "La Femme Nouvelle"

MADAME HODA SCHRAURI PASHA
President of the "Ladies' Wafd"
Honorary President of "La Femme Nouvelle"

MLLE. SENNIA RIAZ PASHA
In Circassian costume

MADAME AMINA BEY SIDKY
President of "La Femme Nouvelle"

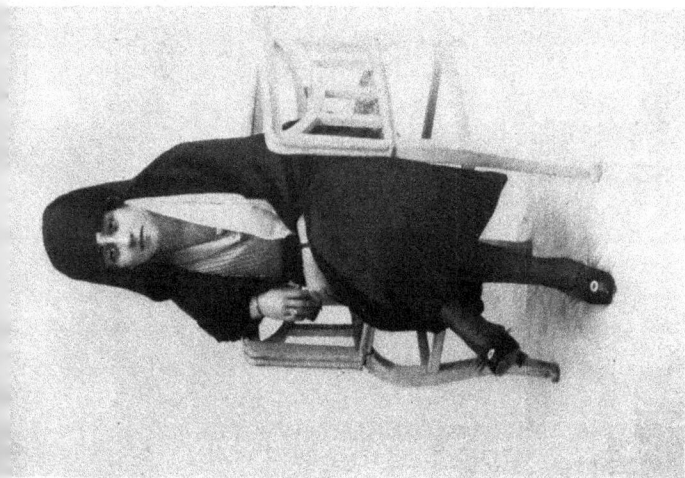

MADAME YOUSSEF BEY GHALI
President of the "Girls' Club of the New Woman"

ABDIN PALACE, CAIRO
The Gilded Cage of the Royal Captive

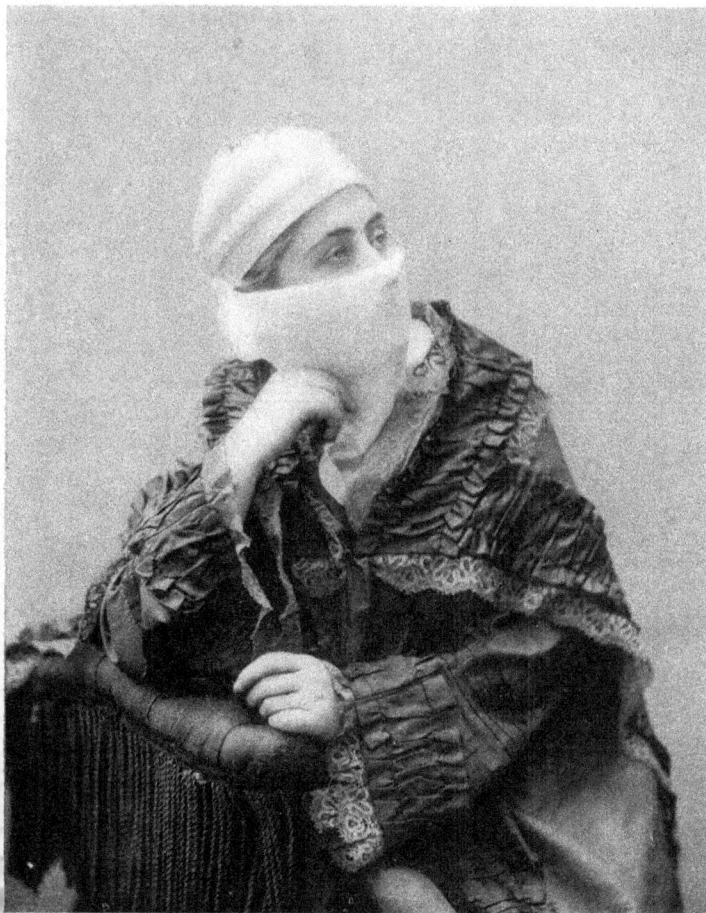

A TURKISH GENTLEWOMAN
The type of Queen Nazli's Grandmother

Publishers' Photo Service

FUAD I, KING OF EGYPT

The king's name was Ahmed Fuad Pasha before he
became Sultan. Now he has been proclaimed king.

ON THE PLEASANT NILE

THE FELLAH WOMAN'S CLUB

A TYPICAL EGYPTIAN GROUP

An Arabian woman wearing the *Yashmak;* her husband in *Galabeyeh* and the son's head well-covered—not forgetting the donkey with its decorated necklace.

A YOUNG EGYPTIAN WOMAN
Of the Old Order (bourgeois class)

THE AMERICAN MISSION SCHOOL GIRLS
On parade at Luxor in honor of the king.

KING FUAD'S DAHABEYEH AT LUXOR

IN THE CHAPEL
American Mission for Girls at Luxor

SITT ESSA
Rescued slave girl
Now cook at the American Mission

[285]

MOTHER AND DAUGHTER
Bringing freshly baked bread
to the American Mission

WOMEN OF THE SUDAN
Showing the slave marks on right cheeks

THE OFFICIAL ENTRY OF FIELD MARSHAL LORD ALLENBY INTO
JERUSALEM THROUGH THE JAFFA GATE ON DECEMBER 11, 1917

EGYPTIAN WOMEN OF THE LOWER CLASS

THE TEMPLE OF ANCIENT GLORY AT LUXOR

THE SUCCULENT, SEDUCTIVE SUGAR CANE

SHEHATA (on the camel)
The Captain of our Caravan

OFF FOR THE PETRIFIED FOREST

"Artelia" looking very temperamental: the Poet and "George Washington" not "speaking" to
each other; Shehata mounted on "Abe Lincoln" and a side-saddle.

THE GRAND OUTER COURT OF THE TEMPLE AT EDFU

Where Rahotep, the High Priest, watched Meral dance, and where
she bade farewell to freedom

HALL OF ILLUMINATION
Up which King Sethron had to levitate himself
(*Illustration from "Ancient Egypt" by George Rawlinson, M. A.*)

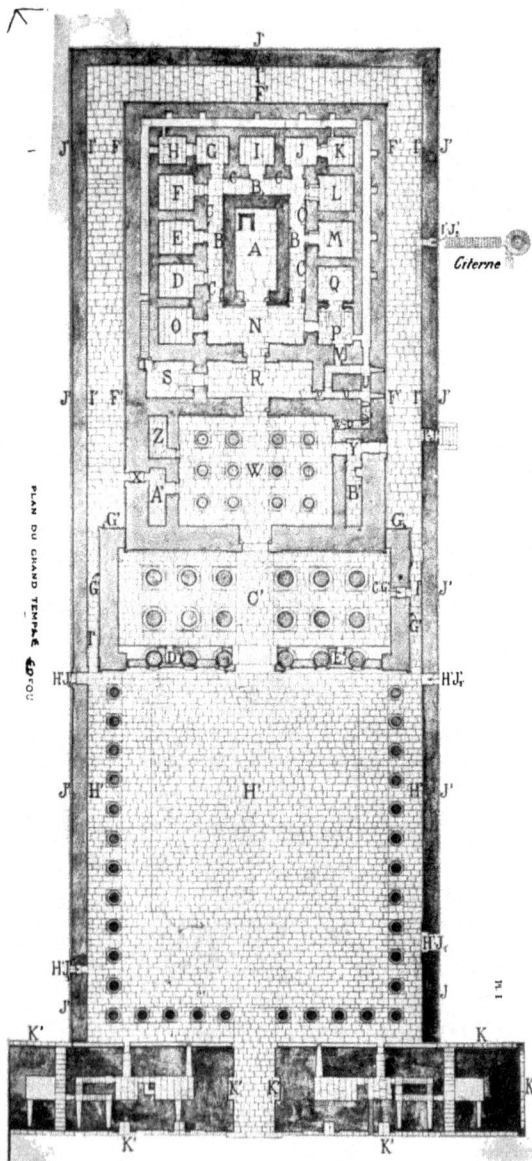

PLAN OF BIBLE TEMPLE

[295]

Seen in the vision of Meral the Priestess

"A"—Holy of Holies   al prayed before statue of
"W." "U." "V." etc.—Priest.   God

THE GREAT TEMPLE AT DENDERAH (RESTORED)

[296]

THOMAS COOK
Founder of Thomas Cook & Son

www.ingramcontent.com/pod-product-compliance
Lightning Source LLC
Chambersburg PA
CBHW072338090426
42741CB00012B/2837